The Welsh Grand Slam 2012

Paul Rees is the vastly respected rugby correspondent for *The Guardian* and the highly acclaimed author of *Glam Slam!: Year of the Dragon* (2005) and *The Resurrection Men: Wales's Grand Slam 2008.*

The Welsh Grand Slam 2012

How Wales Won the Six Nations Championship

PAUL REES

MAINSTREAM
PUBLISHING

EDINBURGH AND LONDON

First published in Great Britain in 2012 by
MAINSTREAM PUBLISHING COMPANY
(EDINBURGH) LTD
7 Albany Street
Edinburgh EH1 3UG

ISBN 9781780575001

A catalogue record for this book is available
from the British Library

Printed in Great Britain by
CPI Group (UK) Ltd, Croydon, CR0 4YY

1 3 5 7 9 10 8 6 4 2

In memory of my mother, Janet, who died on
12 February, the day Wales played Scotland in the
2012 Six Nations.

Acknowledgements

THE AUTHOR THANKS THE FOLLOWING FOR THEIR help in the preparation of this book: Andrew Baldock, the rugby union correspondent of the Press Association, who was unstinting in his help and advice no matter what the hour; Ian Prior, Claire Tolley, Matthew Hancock, Robert Kitson and Mike Averis of *The Guardian* and *The Observer*; Owen Sheers; Andy Selby of 2-halves, the official data suppliers for the RBS Six Nations; Shane Williams, whose predictions are as accurate as his finishing was in the red of Wales; Corris Thomas, the International Rugby Board's head of game analysis; the Arts Council of Wales; the Australian Rugby Union; and Bill Campbell and Ailsa Bathgate at Mainstream Publishing.

Contents

Wales's Grand Slam 2012

5 FEBRUARY 2012	Ireland 21 Wales 23 (Aviva Stadium)
12 FEBRUARY 2012	Wales 27 Scotland 13 (Millennium Stadium)
25 FEBRUARY 2012	England 12 Wales 19 (Twickenham)
10 MARCH 2012	Wales 24 Italy 3 (Millennium Stadium)
17 MARCH 2012	Wales 16 France 9 (Millennium Stadium)

2012 RBS Six Nations Table

TEAM	P	W	D	L	F	A	PTS
1. Wales	5	5	0	0	109	58	10
2. England	5	4	0	1	98	71	8
3. Ireland	5	2	1	2	12	94	5
4. France	5	2	1	2	101	86	5
5. Italy	5	1	0	4	53	121	2
6. Scotland	5	0	0	5	56	108	0

Introduction

WALES'S THIRD GRAND SLAM IN EIGHT SEASONS generated comparisons with the 1970s, when the feat had last been achieved. There was, to me, a significant difference. The current squad is closer to the 1971 team that won the grand slam rather than the 1978 side which completed the clean sweep that decade, because so many players are in the early part of their careers, as the likes of Mervyn Davies, J.P.R. Williams, Gareth Edwards and Gerald Davies were then. This is not the end of an era, more the beginning of one.

When I retired from international rugby at the end of 2011, I appreciated I was leaving a squad that was destined for great things. I am not saying that I knew they would win the grand slam, but there was no doubt we were the side in the Six Nations best equipped to achieve the feat. It all boiled down to the first game in Dublin, when we were up against an Ireland team intent on revenge for the World Cup quarter-final defeat three months before. They were also buoyed by the performances of their provinces in the Heineken Cup, and we went to the Aviva Stadium without half of the first-choice pack.

The Welsh Grand Slam 2012

It was going to be the biggest test of the Six Nations for Wales, and the task was made harder when Sam Warburton did not appear for the second half. In past years, Wales would have folded: that was a time when we had the talent but not the mental strength to go with it. Time and again, we would lose our way at vital moments in tight matches, but that afternoon in Dublin everyone saw a different Wales. The talent was there, as was shown in all of our three tries, but it was supplemented by attitude. I am sure Ireland did not envisage losing a six-point lead in the final five minutes, but Wales not only had the stamina to keep going but also the belief that they would win. The attitude was a legacy of the training camps we had in Poland before the World Cup, when we were pushed to the limits of our endurance.

I had never trained so hard in my life, but as well as making you physically fitter, the two weeks we spent in Spala made us mentally stronger as individuals and drew us together as a squad: we became mates who would do whatever it took to bring each other through, and you saw that in the closing stages in Dublin. At the very point people thought Wales would crack, the players drew on their innermost reserves and pulled through. It was the same at Twickenham, and in the final match against France, tight though it was, there was never a moment when I did not think we would prevail. The blend of desire and belief was obvious, and we thoroughly deserved to win the grand slam.

It was strange watching the games from the commentary box. When the players were warming up, I wanted to be out there and be a part of it again, but I made the right decision to retire. Wales did not miss me, and Alex Cuthbert, who took my place, had an outstanding tournament, scoring three tries and constantly looking to get involved. He showed how our strength in depth has developed in the last couple of years. A number of players who were not regulars in the starting line-up in the Six Nations made a contribution: Rhys Gill, Scott Williams, Justin Tipuric and James Hook are guys who would walk into other sides. And there was Ryan Jones, who covered for absentees in the opening two matches before dropping back onto the bench and coming on in the final three matches to make a huge impact. When Ryan lost the captaincy in 2010, there were questions about whether his international career was coming to an end, but his response was to train even harder and his form has been as good as ever. His attitude sums up what Wales are about: you put your personal disappointment to one side for the good of the cause and it is one reason why Wales are so hard to beat now.

I am not going to put pressure on the players by predicting years of success. They have the potential both to become the team to beat in the Six Nations for seasons to come and to take the next step and beat the top countries in the world, starting with the three-Test series in Australia in the summer. It will be a fascinating match-up with the Wallabies, and it is a long time since Wales have gone on a major tour armed as much with expectation as with hope. The test of attitude will come when we lose a game again, and that will happen at some point. It is all about bouncing back quickly, and the players showed in winning the grand slam after the pain of losing the World Cup semi-final that they have the capacity to turn pain into gain.

Wales's success is down in no small measure to the management team led by Warren Gatland, who has joined a select band of coaches with two grand slams on his CV. I have a huge amount of respect for him, having been in his squad for four years. I looked on him more as a friend than a boss, and he has a special way of managing

15

players. You know he is in charge, but he involves the whole squad, coming up with suggestions and asking for feedback. There has been criticism in the past of Wales's style of play, but rugby is about winning and finding different ways of succeeding, as the All Blacks have shown over the years. Wales were good to watch in the Six Nations, and it was fascinating to see the different way they approached each game. What remained the same was the attitude: focused and unswerving. It was clear after Dublin that it would take a lot to stop Wales winning the grand slam, and hard though England tried at Twickenham, a ground where we have not enjoyed much success over the years, we had the answers.

Wales are in a better place than they have been since the third grand slam in the 1970s. That was the end of a golden period in Welsh rugby; we are at the beginning of one now.

Shane Williams, April 2012

1
The Colden Era

Ability is what you are capable of doing. Motivation determines what you do. Attitude determines how well you do it.

Raymond Chandler

AS THE CROWD LEFT TWICKENHAM AT THE END OF Wales's second victory there in 24 years in the third round of the 2012 RBS Six Nations, they were treated to the unusual sight of the Wales squad, in various states of dress or undress, walking across the concourse and into the car park on the west side of the ground. The players had just done a lap of honour, showing off the triple crown trophy to the many thousands of Wales supporters who were among the capacity 82,000 attendance, but they were not able to linger. They had to look for a converted police van – the only one of its kind in Britain – and step into it, one at a time, for three minutes of torture. It contained a cryotherapy chamber where the temperature was between minus 120 and 160 °C. The treatment was ostensibly an aid to physical recovery, but it also had the effect, starting in a Spartan training camp in Poland the team had visited the previous summer in preparation for the World Cup, of strengthening the players mentally, pushing them to the limits of their endurance and beyond.

The Welsh Grand Slam 2012

The Wales coach Warren Gatland organised two training weeks in Poland in July 2011. The venue was the Poland Olympic Sports Centre in Spala, a remote village 65 miles south of Warsaw with a population of just 400. It is surrounded by forest in one of the largest wooded areas in the country and offers no distractions. The facility's website suggests clients exploit some of the tourist attractions in the area, such as the Skansen Museum of the Pilica River in Tomaszow Mazowiecki, the Farming Centre of Aurochses in Smardzewice, the Entrenchment of Hubal in Anielin or the Barocco Basilica. The Wales squad would have neither the time nor the energy to take in such delights, and by the time they returned home after the second visit they had scratched Poland from their list of potential holiday destinations, although they were to return there before the 2012 Six Nations for a week in snowy Gdansk.

Gatland had used the facilities in Spala when he was the coach of Ireland between 1998 and 2001, and when, after his contract was not renewed, he became the Wasps' director of rugby. The World Cup year offered him the first chance since he had taken over from Gareth Jenkins at the end of 2007 to have his squad together for a significant period of time. He had won a grand slam at the first attempt but, like 2005, it had not been built on a firm foundation. If not quite a happy accident, it developed a momentum all of its own after an unlikely second-half comeback in the opening match against England at Twickenham. Wales went on to defeat Australia the following November and started the 2009 Six Nations with victories over Scotland and England, but they were edged out by France in Paris, ending a sequence of eight successive victories in the tournament, and narrowly lost the final game in Cardiff against an Ireland side that claimed a first grand slam since 1948. The following year, they lost to England at Twickenham, collapsing during the ten minutes the second row Alun Wyn Jones was in the sin-bin for tripping the hooker Dylan Hartley, paid for profligacy at home to France and gave their most passive display under Gatland in losing to Ireland at Croke Park.

The gains of 2008 were being dissipated and there were signs that players were becoming unsettled by Gatland's honesty. As a New Zealander, he was used to saying what he thought and not wrapping his words in euphemisms. His immediate reaction to Jones's yellow card was to accuse the player on television of costing Wales the match: it was an opinion supported by fact as the score was tied at 3–3 when he went to the sin-bin on 34 minutes and 20–3 to England when he returned. 'It was a stupid act and probably cost us the game,' said Gatland. 'We've got to be up front and honest with him: you need 15 players on the pitch.'

The following November, after Wales had drawn against Fiji at the Millennium Stadium, Gatland finished his post-match media conference and was walking out of the door when he turned back to announce that he had taken the captaincy away from Ryan Jones and given it to the hooker Matthew Rees. He was criticised for having a knee-jerk reaction, not least because Jones had given away the penalty that allowed Fiji to tie the match, but said that he had informed Jones's region, Ospreys, earlier in the week about his decision, which he had made because Jones had started to be used by his region in the second row and could no longer be regarded as an automatic starter in the Wales back row. Jones had been the captain throughout Gatland's two years in charge, dedicated and professional, but Wales were on the ebb with less than a year to go before the World Cup. Fiji was their eleventh international in 2010 and their only two victories had come against the two weakest teams in the Six Nations, Scotland and Italy, and Wales only defeated the Scots after staging a remarkable comeback in the final minutes at the Millennium Stadium when the visitors had been reduced to thirteen men. Wales had twice squandered winning positions against South Africa in Cardiff and they were to finish the year by going down at home to the All Blacks 37–25. When England won at the Millennium Stadium on the opening night of the 2011 Six Nations, Wales went to Scotland the following weekend with a record of two wins in their last fourteen internationals and Gatland, for the first time since he had taken charge, was under pressure.

The Welsh Rugby Union had in October 2010 rewarded him with a new contract that would take him to the end of the 2015 World Cup, a change from the governing body's habitual policy of sacking the coach in the build-up to the tournament. Not since the inaugural World Cup in 1987 had Wales been led by a coach who was in position two years before the start of the event. They used four coaches in the four seasons before the 1991 event; they parted company with Alan Davies months before the start of the 1995 World Cup; Graham Henry was hired thirteen months before the 1999 tournament, which the WRU was hosting, started; Steve Hansen had been in charge for eighteen months in 2003, the same time Gareth Jenkins had been in place when Wales went to France in 2007. The prospects, historically, of Gatland leading Wales to his home country were not strong and results increased the pressure from outside on the Union. The former Wales second row Gareth Llewellyn articulated the thoughts of many when he said on BBC Wales: 'The biggest question in the squad is over Warren. His success is built on playing the game a certain way. When he was the coach of Wasps, it was built on a fantastic pack and a team that was much better than anything else out there. He played a particular system that worked and he's carried that on. What Warren has built his success on is not going to sustain us at international level. We have probably got the best set of players any Welsh coach has ever had, but relative to the opposition we are not that much better than anyone else. We play in bursts, when we get desperate and think the game's gone away from us and we start having to play more.'

Back in June, Gatland had predicted that Wales were on the verge of another golden era, three decades after the last one. Ospreys had won the Magners League and Cardiff Blues had become the first Welsh side to enjoy success in European competition when they defeated Toulon at the Stade Vélodrome in Marseille to take the Amlin Challenge Cup. Wales's grand slams in 2005 and 2008 had been achieved without the regions making much impact, success not coming from the bottom up, perhaps one reason why it had not been sustained. 'I honestly feel that between now and the next two World Cups could be a real golden era for Welsh rugby,' said Gatland. 'We have got exciting and talented youngsters coming through, while physically we have a number of players who are in really good shape. This squad is as strong as Wales have had for a few years.'

His vision seemed remote after a troubled autumn international campaign in 2010, one that left the WRU scrambling for position with websites comparing the decision to offer Gatland a new contract unfavourably with Ireland agreeing a new four-year deal with Eddie O'Sullivan before the 2007 World Cup, only to part company with him less than a year later after failure to reach the quarter-finals was followed by a poor Six Nations campaign, and with the Football Association's desperation to retain Fabio Capello beyond the 2010 World Cup in South Africa, which left it in a position where it could not afford to sack the Italian after a series of limp displays culminating in a humiliating defeat to Germany. 'Madness,' wrote one supporter. 'Has the WRU not learned from the FA and Capello? I feel it is short-sighted to be talking to Warren Gatland about a new contract. Current form isn't exactly brilliant: three wins in ten games is not something I would be looking to offer a long-term contract on.'

The WRU pointed out, forcefully, after the draw with Fiji that were Wales to flop in the World Cup, which translated as failing to make the quarter-finals for the fourth time in seven tournaments, it would be able to afford to sack Gatland, whose contract was reported to be worth £1 million before bonuses. It stressed that it had insisted on a one-way release clause that would allow it to part company with the head coach before his new contract started if performances did not match expectations. It was a smart move: not only did the Union reinforce Gatland's position at a time when he had started to look vulnerable, it ensured that it would not lose him should Wales go a long way in the World Cup.

As it turned out, New Zealand needed a new head coach at the end of 2011, with Graham Henry retiring after getting hold of the Webb Ellis Cup at the third attempt. Gatland, who had played for and coached Waikato, was regarded as one of the leading contenders, and a number of former All Blacks urged the New Zealand Rugby Union to approach him, but having lost some £4 million in income that year because of the World Cup, it was in no position to pay the WRU compensation. If, in October 2010, there was a less than enthusiastic response in Wales to another four years of Gatland, there was concern twelve months later that he would, after guiding Wales to the semi-final, look to return home. He did not, unlike his employers, have a break clause, although his new contract did contain a paragraph that allowed him to take a five-month sabbatical should he accept an invitation to become the Lions' head coach on the 2013 tour to Australia.

The Colden Era

As the 2011 Six Nations loomed, Gatland was secure in his job, at least until the end of the World Cup that October. It was less a vote of confidence by the WRU, given the break clause, than a declaration that it would not be jerking its knees before the tournament. It gave Gatland the authority he perhaps needed in the dressing-room, and he changed the way he had been running the squad. Injuries had been a problem for Wales since winning the 2008 grand slam: as an example, Gethin Jenkins, Matthew Rees and Adam Jones had formed the Lions' front row on the 2009 tour to South Africa but since returning had started only three matches together for Wales. Attitude was another issue, with Wales seeming to find various ways of losing.

When Gatland first arrived, he organised everything with military precision: players who had been close to mutiny under the previous set-up responded to being told what to do and when, but a consequence of Gatland speaking his mind publicly and upsetting the sensibilities of some of his charges was that the coach became more inclusive, encouraging input from players. He still had the final word, but he was to find out what Nigel Davies, Wales's attack coach between 2006 and 2007, had already learned to his cost. Welsh players, said Davies, responded best to being told what to do; the more latitude they were given, the less effective they were. After two years of a slow but steady decline, Gatland went back to doing it his way.

'It will be a hard-nosed attitude from now,' said Gatland in an interview with *The Guardian* in January 2011. 'I will tell the players ahead of the Six Nations and the World Cup that at times we have done this and been inclusive, taking their views on board. But now it is a case of "Boys, this is the way it is. If you don't like it, you know where the door is." The problem with professional sport sometimes is that if you have a group of players and ask what you

23

could do for them, they will always want the easier, softer or shorter option, never harder. You have to remind yourself about that and push them, which is when we have been successful in the past. We will push them hard. I spoke recently to someone who had coached Wales and he said that if he had his chance again, he would make different decisions and not compromise: this is the way it will be done. I am very mindful of that.'

Asked about his post-match comment on Alun Wyn Jones's yellow card at Twickenham, he replied: 'I expressed my frustration, saying publicly what everyone else thought, and I know he was disappointed at the time but he learned from the experience and it has made him stronger. If you say nothing, you get criticised for not being honest. You do not win.'

He also talked about the pressure he was facing. 'You are always under pressure,' he said. 'The conclusion I have come to is that you know you are under pressure, but I have to make sure I do not regret any decisions I make and that I do not compromise in what I believe because I might feel under a bit of pressure. I will not compromise on selection, gameplan or style because of politics. You have to be strong and not make decisions you think will be best for your position. When you announce a squad, it always tends to be about who is *not* in rather than who *has* been selected. I have seen others worry about what the media, the [WRU] board and the public are going to say; when you start bowing to that, you are finished. Rugby followers in Wales are incredibly passionate and knowledgeable about the game. They recognise we are not far away. People I know in New Zealand say the same thing. I try and take the emotional side out of it. A number of teams in the world will not want to play Wales at full strength. We have a tough World Cup pool but we will be in great shape by the time the tournament starts. If we can beat South Africa in the first game, we can win that pool. The Springboks will only play one way: territory, scrum and lineout. Have they stuck with their team for too long?'

Gatland touched on a subject that he would address in the summer. 'A frustrating thing for me as a coach is the limited preparation time you have with the players,' he said. 'You do not go through a pre-season. The players this week came in on the Monday when two of the regions had played the previous day. It's a recovery session, you look at organisation the next day, and Thursday and Friday are the first rugby sessions; then you are into match week and have to be up to speed for the first match in the Six Nations. Everyone is under the same pressure and you have to believe in your ability as a coach. I know we are competitive but what is exciting is that we will have the players for two months before the World Cup. That will be like a pre-season and it will make a massive difference. We can go into finer details, whereas this month we have to prioritise. The players know that when they get it right we are not too far away. Wayne Smith [the New Zealand attack coach] said after the All Blacks game, which we need to take on board as players and coaches, that when they play Wales they know that for 65 minutes they are in for one hell of a game. They don't know when that 65 minutes will come, but if they keep their patience and concentration someone will make a crucial mistake to give them an opportunity. That is a good assessment of where we are at. It is an intangible as a coach: you make people aware of it, but players have to go through the experience and learn.'

It was against that backdrop that Gatland arranged to take his players to Spala. The 2011 Six Nations was an improvement on the year before, but only to the extent that Ireland were defeated in Cardiff. England had already won at the Millennium Stadium and while Wales recovered to win their next three games they finished the campaign with a 28–9 defeat against France in Paris. They went into the game with a mathematical chance of winning the title after England's defeat in Dublin earlier in the day, but what victory would have given them was the best record of any side in the Six Nations in the four years since the 2007 World Cup.

Their next match was against the Barbarians at the beginning of June at the Millennium Stadium, an afternoon that again saw Wales snatch defeat when victory had looked theirs. With Gavin Henson, who had resumed playing earlier in the season after taking an eighteen-month sabbatical, making his first international appearance for more than two years, Wales were leading 28–19 with five minutes to go, only to concede two late tries. The players were given a few weeks off before reporting back for the start of World Cup training, and they were given a hint by Gatland of what they could expect in Spala.

'The first camp is going to be very physical,' he said. 'Players will be training two or three times a day in the gym and out on the field. A number of fitness staff are going, and the players will find it really tough. I have been there before with Ireland and Wasps, and we got some great results from it. The players will work really hard.' He went on, with words that would be better appreciated after Wales had qualified from their World Cup group: 'When you have been to Spala and gone through some of the pain that is out there it develops that mental toughness you are looking for. I hope the players have a few memories from the camp they can look back on and draw from in the World Cup. If we are under pressure in matches or hammering away towards the end of games, they will be able to turn to each other and push each other on, saying, "Remember the agony we went through in Poland and how hard we worked?" It is not a five-star luxury hotel. It is a fairly basic place, but the facilities for sports people are excellent. We are looking for honest, hardworking people who are prepared to put their bodies on the line. The characteristic of a good World Cup tourist is someone who is selfless.'

The Spala centre opened in 2000, but Wales's strong showing in the 2011 World Cup generated considerable publicity for its cryotherapy division after Warburton described the sub-zero chamber as an 'evil sauna'. The physical benefit of using cryotherapy was that it aided recovery by reducing inflammation. 'It dampens the nervous system,' said Adam Beard, Wales's head of physical performance. 'It gives you that painless feel. It allows you to flush toxins away from the working muscles pretty quickly because you're in extreme temperatures and the blood wants to move away from the limbs to regulate the core temperature. Once you get out, there's a feeling of freshness. That's the endorphins rushing through your system. We use it around a training programme we've adapted for the last four or five years. Cryotherapy's not magic. A number of people are asking why are we letting the cat out of the bag. Isn't it our trade secret? I don't think it is. We use it around a training programme we've adapted for the last four or five years.'

During the 2012 Six Nations, Beard explained to the *Daily Mail* one of the reasons Gatland had wanted to go to Spala: 'The big thing for Warren when I took over [in 2009] was that he felt we weren't able to play the game we wanted to. My first job was to ensure the players were able to do that. We tried to go away from a lot of the traditional methods of strength and conditioning and find methods that actually helped rugby. We involve players, too. When they come off after a Test match, we'll ask them how they felt during certain moments. Guys like Alun Wyn Jones have helped invent exercises and fitness drills that we've incorporated. There are a number of boys who are very impressive in the gym, but we've tried to give them a little more scope. Dan Lydiate's leg used to blow up after 50 or 60 minutes, and we've worked really hard at getting his running economy sorted and his ability to finish games in a fit state. We felt before the World Cup that we weren't as "running fit" as we would like to be, so we got someone to help us out with a better running economy. We were chewing up energy and when you do that you're going to get smaller players. The body cannot physically eat enough – our food bill is astronomical and we feed the boys five or six times a day – so we use supplements to aid recovery and help manufacture big, lean and fit players. Cryotherapy is a buzzword but it is not the be-all and end-all. The boys go through a lot of pain, physically and mentally, then the cryotherapy complements that. If you just chuck someone into a chamber and expect a result then you are kidding yourself.'

It was far removed from the 1970s when the word cold meant something different to players: the temperature of the bottles of beer chilling in the dressing-room at the end of a match. When Wales defeated England at Twickenham at the start of the 1978 grand slam, few players lingered on the field. Their concern was not finding where the mobile cryotherapy chamber was parked. 'You had to get in quick before the free beer ran out,' said one former Wales and Lions player. 'As soon as the match ended you were on the lash. Rugby was a social game then, but we must have been fit because there were no mass substitutions in those days: you stayed on the field for the whole match unless you were badly injured and we played twice a week for most of the year.'

It was an era when Wales married ability with motivation

and attitude; club rugby was then strong and seasons were stuffed with local derbies. Mental hardness was a given in Welsh players; it was not an environment where the weak survived. As another 1970s international observed in the week of the 2012 grand slam match against France, 'A difference between the two eras is that in the 1970s you were picked for Wales on the strength of your club performances; now it is down to how you perform in training.'

At the start of 2011, Gatland found himself standing at a crossroads. He had remarked weeks after starting work with Wales that, in terms of natural ability, the country was richer than New Zealand. The difference was that at crucial points in a Test match the All Blacks would invariably impose themselves and make a decisive play, while Wales would, at the moment of reckoning, usually falter. The 2009 meeting between the sides in Cardiff offered an example: Wales were trailing 19–12 with three minutes to go when Alun Wyn Jones intercepted a pass from the scrum-half Jimmy Cowan on the New Zealand 22. The lock had no one in front of him when he set off; had it been Shane Williams or Leigh Halfpenny, the home side's two wings that day, in possession, Wales would have avoided defeat to the All Blacks for the first time in fifty-six years, but Jones realised, after he had covered half the distance to the opposition line, that he was not going to make it. As he weighed up his options and worked out who to pass to, the wing Zac Guildford had tracked back and deflected the ball away from danger. 'I should have done a lot better,' said Jones. 'I turned in but I did not see Guildford coming across. If I had gone on the outside, I would have gone a bit further towards the line. World-class players finish things like that and I do not think it was a world-class instance in the game for myself. Will I take responsibility? Yes, that's what international players do. Will I blame anyone? No. It was a critical moment we did not nail. We will keep getting the tag of nearly men, but that is going to come to an end sooner or later. When it does I hope I am around.'

If Jones was hard on himself – and worse was to come for him at Twickenham three months later – his words would have resonated with Gatland and heartened the coach, but as 2010 yielded even more disappointment than the year before a question the coach reflected on was whether years of near misses had left the squad scarred by failure. His own shock tactics, such as plain speaking, were not having the impact he expected.

Gatland had never been afraid to promote young players. When he was in charge of Ireland, he had given a first cap to Brian O'Driscoll. The centre was 20 and had only been playing for Leinster for a few months. Wales's World Cup squad in 2011 would feature a core of young players who were little known in the wide rugby world, many of whom had been promoted by Gatland when they were not regular starters for their regions. When Wales went to Twickenham in the 2012 Six Nations, there were only three survivors from the starting line-up two years previously: Jamie Roberts, Adam Jones and Alun Wyn Jones. It was a mixture of the infusion of young blood and the bonding in adversity in Poland that gave Wales renewed momentum, as the wing Shane Williams had acknowledged.

Williams had first been capped by Wales in 2000 and had played under seven different national coaches: Graham Henry, Steve Hansen, Mike Ruddock, Scott Johnson, Gareth Jenkins, Nigel Davies and Gatland. He was used to the boom-and-bust culture of Welsh rugby – a soaring high followed by an intense low – but he quickly detected something different about the 2011 squad as he shivered in the cryotherapy chamber in Spala and found himself getting up voluntarily for training sessions at 4 a.m. Williams, who was to retire from international rugby at the end of the year, two months before his 35th birthday, had long believed that Wales had the potential to beat the best teams in the world and struggled to explain why near misses continued to follow each other. When he returned from the second training camp in Poland, he was aware that there had been a fundamental change in the mindset of the players.

'The first thing that struck me was that the young players had no fear of failure,' said Williams. 'Early on in the camp, Sam Warburton and George North said that we were going to win the World Cup, and they were not joking. That attitude proved infectious and spread to the older players like myself. Poland had a lot to do with hardening attitudes. It brought us close together as a squad because we suffered together. A lot has been said about cryotherapy, but you found out a lot about yourself. There are two compartments to the chamber in Spala. The first one is basically a fridge you go into to acclimatise and then a main door is opened and you step into minus 140°C for three of the longest minutes I have ever experienced. You really had to dig in, standing up, moving around and occupying yourself as best as you could. You keep talking to each other, but it gets very difficult. You lose concentration in that temperature and find yourself talking nonsense half the time. The overall training was the toughest I had been involved in, and I was absolutely shattered when I got home. We had been to hell and back and were stronger for the experience.

'The complex in Spala was nice enough, and it was not like being in prison, but it was in the middle of nowhere and there was nothing to do. It was not a place you would choose to go for a holiday. There were other athletes there, and we watched a few wrestling bouts, but we were there to work. We shared rooms that were on the small side. A number of players were in the squad for the first time and I did not know many of them. I did by the end of our stay in Poland: we had to pitch in together to get through the experience. I do not think it was any coincidence that in every match in the 2012 Six Nations Wales looked the stronger side on the hour mark, the time when fatigue starts to kick in. Poland was a big reason for that: yes, we were physically fit and supremely conditioned, but Wales were stronger mentally. When the players were having to dig in in the final minutes, their minds would have gone back to Spala and Gdansk, where they were pushed to the limits of their endurance, and those experiences helped them pull through.'

After Wales's opening victory in the 2012 Six Nations, when they came from six points behind with five minutes to go to defeat Ireland in Dublin, Halfpenny questioned whether it was a match Wales would have won without their experiences in Poland. 'It was a harsh environment that tested you mentally,' he said. 'It was like a military camp, pushing you to breaking point. There were no home comforts during our trips to Poland: the rooms were basic, no nice beds, and the food was not to our taste – egg with everything. No one there spoke our language. It was just us, and when we were there last month it was freezing cold. We trained on the beach and it was covered in snow. You made sure that you did not give in and pulled others through. There were times when you felt like giving up: you thought you had no more to offer and then, from somewhere, you found an extra bit. That is what it was like in Dublin in the last five minutes when we were behind and had a player in the sin-bin. Your mind is drained and you need the support of your teammates to lift you and pull you through, making sure we all get to the finishing line. Every single player contributed to winning the match. It was a really hard game, and 75 minutes in you felt as you had in Poland: you had to look deep inside yourself to be able to get the result and we knew, because of what we had been through together, that we had the character to do it.'

As Halfpenny spoke, in his quiet, understated manner, he reflected on the new Wales. He had been shattered after the World Cup semi-final defeat to France: his late, long-distance penalty, which would have won the match, dropped underneath the crossbar. A breath of wind in the Auckland night would have taken the ball over, but, instead of preparing for the final, Wales again had to reflect on what could, and should, have been. It was the sort of heart-wrenching defeat that in the past would have played on their minds for a long while afterwards, sapping energy. Halfpenny could barely speak in the hours after the defeat to France and he was still inconsolable a few days later, but as Wales gathered to prepare for the 2012 Six Nations he was looking forward, not back. 'We want to be the best,' he said. 'That means winning every game and claiming the grand slam. That is the objective for this tournament, nothing less. We are preparing exactly as we did in the World Cup, another tournament we set out to win. We set our aims high and want to be the best. Winning trophies is our goal and we believe we are good enough to succeed in that.'

Halfpenny delivered. There were 30 minutes to go of Wales's final match in the 2012 Six Nations against France in Cardiff when he lined up a penalty a few metres inside his own half. Wales were leading 10–6 in a tense encounter, but Les Bleus were enjoying their best period of the afternoon. The kick was almost in front of the posts, as the late penalty had been in the Auckland semi-final. It was some eight metres longer, but Halfpenny quickly stepped up to claim the ball after Lydiate had won the penalty with another of his trademark tackles. He was not thinking of redemption for what happened at Eden Park, merely putting Wales closer to the grand slam and a trophy. As he went through his routine, his mind went back to his boyhood when he would go with his grandfather, Malcolm, to a field near his home in Gorseinon, Swansea, and practise his goal-kicking, having been inspired to take it up by the exploits of the England outside-half Jonny Wilkinson. 'People ask me how I cope with the pressure and the noise in the stadiums, but I just block it out,' he said two days before the grand slam match against France in an echo of Wales's most prolific points scorer Neil Jenkins, who since 2008 has been the national side's kicking coach. 'I just picture myself on the peaceful training pitch when there is nobody else around: just me, the ball and a set of posts. Since the World Cup semi-final I have said to myself that if I ever get a moment like that, I am going to nail it. There was not a single day that went by when I did not think about that kick. I would have done anything for it to go over, but it has gone. It is history. It is now all about the next one.'

The kick against France in 2012 was not to win the game, but it was still significant. Halfpenny took his time, his mind back in Gorseinon, and the ball cleared the crossbar with something to spare. The full-back, another player plucked from relative obscurity by Gatland when he won his first cap against South Africa in 2008 as a 19 year old, far from bearing the scars of failure, was motivated by success, a quality his teammates shared. Their achievement in coming so close to making the World Cup final had been questioned by some who pointed out that, yet again, Wales had lost tight matches, going down to both South Africa and France by a point, while the only side of note they had beaten was Ireland. The argument missed the point: Wales had undergone a profound change and were no longer a side that habitually lost concentration at vital moments. After the opening group game against the Springboks, they did not concede a try in the final quarter until the play-off match against Australia, when they had been stretched by injuries. It was a different Wales, one varnished by Polish polish.

2

Tipping Point

The prize was right there underneath our eyeballs.
Everybody went low.

John Hiatt

WALES OPENED THEIR 2012 SIX NATIONS CAMPAIGN
in Dublin, their first visit to the Aviva Stadium, as
Lansdowne Road had become. The last time they had
started a campaign in the Irish capital, a decade before,
they had also had a New Zealander at the helm, Graham
Henry. The 54–10 defeat, which followed the 55 points
leaked by Wales in the A international in Cork the previous
day, turned out to be his final match in charge. He resigned
as head coach before the week was out, a bitterly sad end
that contrasted with the strong start he had made. Two of
Wales's management team in 2012, Robert Howley and
Robin McBryde, were in the starting line-up in 2002, while
Ireland's side included the second row Paul O'Connell,
who, ten years later, had succeeded the injured Brian
O'Driscoll as captain. To complete the circle, the 2002
match was Ireland's first in the Six Nations since the Irish
Rugby Football Union had parted company with Warren
Gatland the year before. Now Wales were looking for their
third successive victory over Ireland, something they had

not achieved since the 1970s, while the Irish were fuelled by memories of their last game: the World Cup quarter-final against Wales in Wellington that they lost 22–10 after beating Australia in the pool stage to knock the tournament on its axis and ensure that the final would be contested by teams from the two hemispheres.

France were the pre-tournament favourites, but a flurry of late money was placed on Wales at bookmakers, even though they had been hit by injuries. Gatland delayed naming his side until the Friday before the match, which was being held on the Sunday, because he wanted to give players as long to prove their fitness as he was allowed: under the tournament regulations, starting line-ups had to be announced no later than 48 hours before kick-off.

The final two rounds of European cup action in January had proved costly: the prop Gethin Jenkins sustained a knee ligament injury that threatened to put him out for at least the first two rounds of the Six Nations; the flanker Dan Lydiate aggravated an ankle problem and was regarded as doubtful for Dublin; while the outside-half Rhys Priestland suffered a knee strain playing for the Scarlets. The second rows Alun Wyn Jones and Luke Charteris had already been ruled out with long-term injuries and the hooker Matthew Rees, who had been due to lead Wales in the World Cup, only to have to withdraw from the squad because he needed an operation on his neck, pulled a calf muscle in training. It meant that Wales would be without five forwards, while the centre Jamie Roberts had not played for six weeks because of a knee injury. Not everyone shared the punters' optimism, and not just because of the number of players who were unavailable: Wales had only won in Dublin twice in the Six Nations, and Ireland had not lost an opening match at home in the championship since the days of the old Five Nations.

The Welsh Grand Slam 2012

The former England scrum-half Austin Healey was one of those who said it would not be Wales's year, and he was far from alone. Healey had not endeared himself to Welsh supporters when, during the 2001 Lions tour to Australia, he used his newspaper column to sharply criticise the tourists' head coach, Graham Henry. Two days before the start of the 2012 Six Nations, he questioned what Wales had really achieved in the World Cup a few months before. 'Wales played well in one game, against Ireland,' he said. 'You can make that two, but they lost the other, to South Africa, because they did not have the self-belief to win. I think Wales will struggle in this year's championship because the way the fixtures fall is bad for them. Going to Dublin first up is tough, and I cannot see them winning that one. Ireland are flying with three teams in the knock-out stages of the Heineken Cup and they have a strong squad; I expect them to win by fourteen points. I think Wales will finish fourth in the table with two wins, against Scotland and Italy. France will win it with England second and Ireland third.'

Healey was to become involved in a heated debate on Twitter later in the tournament after posting a message that Leigh Halfpenny should have been sent off for taking out in the air the Italy number 8 Sergio Parisse during the match between the sides at the Millennium Stadium. The Wales full-back received a yellow card and Healey's observation drew a critical response from Welsh supporters, one comparing Healey as a player unflatteringly to Halfpenny, provoking a scatological reply.

One of Healey's concerns pre-tournament was how Wales would cope without Shane Williams, who had retired from Test rugby after 87 caps and a record 58 tries. He pointed out that Wales's generally conservative approach had been leavened by the ability of Williams, one of the more diminutive players in a professional game that was increasingly becoming a land inhabited by giants, to create something out of nothing. He was replaced in the side by Alex Cuthbert, who had started the season as a fringe player with Cardiff Blues, where he was on a development contract worth some £100 a week, a salary supplemented by £14,000 a year as a member of Wales's Sevens squad. The Gloucester-born Cuthbert was, like George North on Wales's other wing, rather bigger in build than Williams at 6 ft 6 in. and 16 st. 5 lb. At the start of the professional era, when Wales tended to lose heavily to the major southern hemisphere nations and suffered record defeats against England and France, their size, or lack of it, was one of the reasons cited for their travails. Wales, it was said, had never been a nation of big players and had had to rely on qualities such as guile and cunning to prevail. Size was a factor in the 2012 Six Nations, but this time Wales were looking down on the rest.

For the first time since 1977, Wales went through a championship campaign with the same starting line-up behind the scrum. Halfpenny was the only player who was less than 6 ft, and then only by a couple of inches. The average height of Wales's backs was 6 ft 2 in., and the average weight was 15 st. 11 lb; England's was 6 ft and 14 st. 4 lb; New Zealand's in the World Cup was 6 ft and 15 st. 2 lb and South Africa's was 6 ft 1 in. and 14 st. 4 lb. Gatland said that he had not consciously opted for size, picking the backs as individuals rather than as a unit. He had earmarked Cuthbert as Williams's replacement during the World Cup after watching videos of the wing playing for the Blues and used him as a replacement in the December 2011 friendly against Australia at the Millennium Stadium. At twenty-one, Cuthbert was two years older than North, who was winning his seventeenth cap against Ireland and had only started playing rugby union when he was sixteen and a student at Hartpury

College. North, who was also born in England, won his first cap when he was eighteen, having made six appearances for the Scarlets. If part of Gatland's motivation in picking him against South Africa in the autumn of 2010 was to make him permanently unavailable to the country of his birth, Cuthbert had already committed himself to the land of his mother Caroline, who was born in Wrexham, by playing on the Sevens circuit. When Wales were doing battle in the 2011 Six Nations, Cuthbert was playing for Cardiff RFC in the semi-professional Welsh Premiership, and in the week that the national squad left for the World Cup in New Zealand he was making his fifth and final appearance for the Blue and Blacks in a pre-season friendly against Bedford. He made his league debut for the Blues on 11 September, and seven appearances later he was called into the Wales squad and named on the bench against the Wallabies.

Cuthbert was an all-round sportsman while at school. He was on the football club Gloucester City's books, he won regularly on show jumping's national circuit and as a 400m runner he clocked national standard times. 'Sport has been my whole life,' he said. 'I had always had a dream of becoming a professional in one sport, but I did not know which one to take on. I travelled around the country for show jumping competitions and I won quite a bit of money. A horse I sold, Neapolitan II, has jumped at the Horse of the Year Show. At the age of 16, I was trying to fit everything in and I was working on the family farm with my father and brother, milking, cleaning the sheds out and doing the usual daily jobs on a farm. I first started playing rugby in the odd Sevens tournament when I was at Hartpury College, and after a summer tournament in Manchester a member of Wales's World Cup-winning Sevens squad, Craig Hill, was there and he contacted the coach Paul John to tell him about me. It all started from there and it is hard to take in what has happened in my career so quickly. At the start of the season, my aim was to get into the Blues squad and play a few games. Appearing in the Six Nations never entered my mind, and I know I still have a lot to work and improve on.'

Cuthbert was to finish the 2012 Six Nations as Wales's leading try scorer, but his debut in the tournament lasted only 40 minutes as a head injury forced him off the field in Dublin at half-time. North lasted rather longer, unfortunately for Ireland, who knew all about him from the World Cup. North, whose family moved to Anglesey when he was five, had been compared to Jonah Lomu, who as a twenty year old took the 1995 World Cup by storm, a player with the speed of a wing and the weight of a prop. North had scored two tries on his debut against South Africa, becoming the first debutant to do so against the Springboks. Injury forced him to miss the first four matches of the 2011 Six Nations, but he became Wales's most talked about player during the World Cup, not just because of his pace and power but because of his willingness to go in search of the ball and his composure. He looked a seasoned international, not someone still in his teens, but after returning from New Zealand he struggled to make an impact with the Scarlets. Three weeks before the start of the Six Nations, he had played in a Heineken Cup match against Northampton at Parc-y-Scarlets and seemed to be struggling with fatigue. He was twice put away only to be hauled down by the full-back and then caught by Tom May, who was not regarded as one of the quicker centres on the English circuit. By the time he went to Dublin, it had been a year since he had scored a try for his region, and he was not the only member of the Wales squad who had not made an impact in Europe – in contrast to Ireland. Munster and Leinster had both topped their Heineken Cup pools with unbeaten records: Munster won their six matches, which included the double over Northampton, while Leinster's one blemish had been a draw in Montpellier. Ulster had also made the last eight and the strength of Ireland's provinces in Europe contrasted with Wales's relative weakness: the Blues qualified for the quarter-finals as one of the best group runners-up, earning them a trip to the holders, Leinster; the Scarlets rallied on the final weekend to claim one of the three spots reserved for Heineken Cup sides in the quarter-finals of the Amlin Challenge Cup, while Ospreys finished third in their pool behind Saracens and Biarritz.

The Heineken Cup had rarely been a reliable barometer. In the previous ten seasons before 2011–12, the same country had only twice provided the winners of the Six Nations and the Heineken Cup: Ireland in 2009 and France a year later. The Ireland squad players based in the country were retained on central contracts, which allowed the national coach Declan Kidney to dictate when they played for their provinces. In contrast, the Wales players were contracted to their regions, although a 2009 agreement between the WRU and the four regions had reduced the friction over issues such as player release that had existed before. The control the Ireland coach exerted over his players meant that they enjoyed longer rest periods than their rivals in England, France and Scotland. Their appearances in the RaboDirect PRO12 tended to be rationed, but they were always made available for the Heineken Cup, a tournament the Irish had come to dominate with Munster's success in 2006 and 2008 followed by Leinster's conquests in 2009 and 2011.

'It is hard not to look across the Irish Sea and feel pangs of envy and puzzlement, given the respective achievements at club level,' wrote Hugh Farrelly, the rugby correspondent of the *Irish Independent* as he reflected on the 2012 Six

Nations. 'Perhaps the best course of action now when pondering Ireland's national selection policy is to ask a simple question: what would Wales do? The [Newport Gwent] Dragons used to be a joke on the Celtic League circuit. Never the most athletic of sides, they would waddle onto the RDS, Musgrave Park or Ravenhill with bright yellow jerseys bulging over their bellies, ripe for another stuffing. You were aware of the names without paying too much attention – the interest lay in how many points they would ship and they never disappointed. They were punchbags and a rugby punchline, but no one is laughing at the Dragons now. Luke Charteris, Toby Faletau and the brilliant Dan Lydiate all play for the club and are the best examples of how Welsh rugby overcomes club deficiencies to flourish at international level. Ireland have been racking up the Heineken Cup titles, four since 2006, but have been unable to turn those achievements into consistency at international level since their grand slam in 2009. The Welsh have had three grand slams to savour since 2005, and though the lack of trophies at club level is a frequent topic of debate, any concern is swamped by the fact that players are coming through to aid the national cause. There is still plenty of young talent in Ireland; the difference between the two countries is the willingness to give it its head while, in key positions, Ireland's pool has been shown to be worryingly shallow.'

One characteristic of Leinster and Munster in Europe was their ability to grind out results, winning matches even when some way below their best. The Welsh regions needed to play at their optimum to win tight Heineken Cup contests, and even then it was not always enough. Watching George North the month before Wales went to Dublin was to perceive a player, for the first time in his short career, struggling for form, and he did not appear to be alone. Few of the World Cup squad had made an impact since returning to their regions, and North admitted that he had not been at his best. 'I was disappointed with the way I had been playing for the Scarlets when I joined up with Wales,' he said before Wales flew to Dublin. 'I suffered a dead leg recently and have been trying to get over that. I had a week off after the World Cup and not much since, but I feel fine. It has been a long season, and I suppose it is only halfway through, but the prospect of playing in the Six Nations gives you a boost. I have not seen much of the ball in recent games for the Scarlets, and you just have to keep working hard. I feel a lot fresher having been to the camp in Poland last week, and you could say the same for a number of the boys. Everyone had a few niggles – you can't go through a season without them – but the cryotherapy in Poland did its job in keeping the body in good shape. We had sessions twice a day and on the last day we had three.'

The Scarlets' head coach Nigel Davies had taken North aside before the Wales squad gathered to start preparing for the Six Nations. 'He had come back from a successful World Cup and things were not happening for him,' he said. 'He felt he had to perform and I told him to relax and enjoy his rugby. He was not going to win us every game, and I wanted to take the pressure off him. He is still not 20, and he will have to endure some troughs, but you also know that his peaks are going to be very, very high. He has so much talent: we have not seen the best of him yet by a long way. He is unique in that he is so aerobically and anaerobically fit. Some players have explosive pace over a short distance, but George keeps going. His size makes him stand out as a wing, but he is very fast and skilful, adept at using his qualities to create opportunities for others as well as to score tries himself. He has achieved so much so quickly, but he is a grounded lad, exceptionally mature for his age. He had only played a couple of games for us when I told Warren Gatland that we had someone who was worth watching. He looked so comfortable.'

Wales were together for two weeks before the opener in Dublin. The first they spent in Gdansk, cold-weather training, although the contingent in the squad who were based in France and England only stayed for three days, as their clubs exercised their rights under the International Rugby Board's regulation governing the release of players for international duty.

The camp in Poland differed from that of the previous summer in one significant sense: the first had been designed to get the players physically and mentally fit for what would be a gruelling tournament, but in Gdansk Gatland appreciated that some of his charges needed to be handled more carefully than others. His career as a coach had been marked by the way he treated players as individuals: what worked for some would not for others. As the 2012 Six Nations campaign progressed, he gave extra time off to the Newport Gwent Dragons number 8 Toby Faletau, a twenty-one year old who had played in every World Cup match and who was a regular in the championship campaign, one of only three forwards to start in all five matches. When he was the director of rugby at Wasps, Gatland eased back in training as a season approached its end, giving players extra days off. It gave them a freshness others lacked at a crucial point in the campaign and it marked the start of a period of success for the club in England and Europe.

'Poland was a really good exercise for us,' said the Wales attack coach Rob Howley at the start of the week building up to the Ireland game. 'It allowed us to concentrate on skills and getting the mindset ready for what will confront us on Sunday afternoon. There was a wind chill factor of minus 13 in Gdansk, and we did not organise many full contact sessions. It was more an MOT of the body, making sure that the boys were freshened up after their matches in Europe for the regions. What we now have is competition for places and that allows us to work on combinations in training, even allowing for the players who were carrying injuries.' With Gethin Jenkins, Luke Charteris and Alun Wyn Jones already ruled out, there was concern that two players who had been a pivotal part of Wales's World Cup campaign, Priestland and Lydiate, would not recover in time to play in Dublin.

Priestland had been one of Wales's unexpected successes in the World Cup. He had made one appearance from the bench in the 2011 Six Nations and was also a replacement against the Barbarians in June. He was seen as more of an option at full-back than his preferred position of outside-half. He tended to play at 15 for the Scarlets, with Stephen Jones at 10. Jones was the longest-serving player in the Wales squad in the World Cup, but he was not involved in the December friendly against Australia and was initially left out of the 2012 Six Nations squad. Jones had vied with James Hook for the Wales outside-half jersey during Gatland's time in charge, seeing off a brief challenge by Dan Biggar, and was chosen at 10 when Wales started their series of World Cup warm-ups against England at Twickenham in August 2011. Hook's versatility, and the fact that he was used by Ospreys as a centre, counted against him with Wales: his preferred position was outside-half and he had started the 2008 grand slam rolling with a shimmying break and deft pass to create a try for Lee Byrne in the opening match at Twickenham, but during the campaign Gatland became caught between the instinctive play of Hook, which occasionally led to mistakes, and the controlling influence of Jones. Hook finished that Six Nations at outside-half, but he only started there twice more for Wales before the 2011 tournament.

Gatland had said privately after Wales had returned from the second training camp in Spala that he could envisage Priestland being Wales's outside-half in the World Cup. He had been taken by the composure and coolness the then 24 year old had shown, together with his competitiveness, but Priestland got his chance by accident. Jones suffered a calf strain in the warm-up at Twickenham, and Priestland, who had been chosen at full-back, was told five minutes before the kick-off that he would be starting at 10. 'I had no time to be nervous,' he said afterwards.

Gatland's instinct had been right, and even though Wales lost 23–19 to England they had finished the game the stronger and Priestland had given an assured performance, bringing his outside-backs into play. Wales had played a narrower game in the Six Nations, but Priestland's ability to see what was on before he received the ball, like the very best midfielders in football, gave him the gift of time. His contribution to the World Cup campaign could be measured in how Wales performed without him: he suffered a shoulder injury during the closing minutes of the quarter-final against Ireland and missed both the semi-final against France and the play-off against Australia, matches in which Wales reverted to a narrower approach.

'My approach has always been to play with my head up, and that is something the coaches at both Wales and the Scarlets encourage,' said Priestland, reflecting on the World Cup campaign before the December friendly against Australia. 'I know I am not the fastest or the strongest, and I just try to read the game, bringing in the players around me. There are times when we have to be direct and get over the gainline, but we cannot be a one-dimensional team. We have to be smart. When I was injured against Ireland, I knew that it was bad news

47

because it was so painful. I could not feel sorry for myself because there were so many players who had not made it to New Zealand. I had been lucky having played in five games in the tournament, more than I had thought I would at the start. The disappointment was in losing to France and Australia: it took away a bit from the way we had played. My goal throughout the summer had been to make the World Cup squad and I had a chance earlier than I was going to when Stephen was injured at Twickenham. I am wiser and more experienced now. It was strange going back to the Scarlets after the World Cup and starting a Heineken Cup game at 10 with Stephen on the bench. It was a position I had not been in before, and it showed how things had changed for me. Stephen has been superb with me, always giving me pointers on how I can improve. He never says anything to put you down but looks to help get the best out of you.

'People have asked me a lot if I feel any pressure because of the regard in which the outside-half position is held in Wales. I try not to put too much pressure on myself. I used to really beat myself up when things did not go right. No one goes out to have a bad game, but I know that, sooner or later, I will have one. Outside-half is simply where I want to play. I like to have the ball in my hands and be the playmaker. You can get frustrated playing at full-back because you spend long periods on your own, but an outside-half can only be as good as the players around him. Wales are much stronger at forward now and it is important that we build on the performances in the World Cup. At the end of it we did lose to South Africa, France and Australia; as a squad we are pretty disappointed with that and we have to learn from the experience going into the game against Australia and next year.'

Priestland was passed fit to play against Ireland and within 15 minutes in Dublin he had created Wales's first try of the campaign, breaking on the blind-side and showing the ball to defenders, waiting for them to commit before passing to the centre Jonathan Davies, who had the space to squeeze in at the corner for the first of his two tries in the match. Ireland had talked before the game about making a strong start, but Wales had already had a try ruled out. Ryan Jones, playing at blind-side flanker in place of Lydiate, forced his way over the line but the television match official Geoff Warren ruled that the forward had been held up.

Jones may have been starting because of injury, but he had remained a key member of the squad despite having been stripped of the captaincy 14 months before. Gatland had placed a premium on players reacting to disappointment by putting the needs of the squad before themselves, but if being dropped is one thing, being removed as captain is another. Jones had led Wales in the 2008 grand slam, but in the following year was left out of the Lions squad for the tour to South Africa. Gatland was part of the management team, along with Howley and the Wales defence coach Shaun Edwards, and the omission of Jones, who had been one of the few players to emerge from the Lions tour to New Zealand with his reputation enhanced after being called out as a replacement and quickly forcing his way into the Test side, generated considerable publicity in Wales. He did make a fleeting visit to South Africa after again being summoned as a replacement, but twenty-four hours after he had arrived in Cape Town he was flying home: he had suffered two knocks to his head during Wales's tour to the United States and Canada, which had just finished. He had to undergo a series of tests in hospital to prove he was fit to play, but he failed them and was sent home.

Wales's strong showing in the World Cup had been credited in the media largely to the coterie of young players who, having come through the academy system run by the WRU, had never been exposed to rugby's traditional beery downtime. 'They have a great work ethic and the time when rugby had a drinking culture is unknown to them,' said Gatland at the end of 2011. 'Their attitude has rubbed off on the older players, and one aspect about our World Cup campaign is that the youngsters feel disappointed, not satisfied. There is a sense of emptiness because we came so close to making the final and they will not, despite the reaction here to what we did in New Zealand, get ahead of themselves. We will make sure of that.'

At thirty, Ryan Jones was one of the most experienced players in the squad and one of the few who had been part of two grand slam campaigns. In him, Gatland could have no better response to personal disappointment.

'Coping with the loss of the captaincy was difficult,' said Jones before Wales left for the World Cup. 'I am not going to lie about that. It is still difficult now. I handled it in my own way: I have a great circle of close family and friends, and they were incredibly supportive. When I was a boy, my father once said to me that you define a man by how he deals with lows in his life. You cannot allow an incident to linger: you have to keep your dignity, deal with it and come out on the other side a better person. The responsibility you have in a squad does not end when you lose the captaincy. You have to make the environment comfortable for young players; it is about putting something back in. I thoroughly enjoy playing rugby and I love playing for Wales. I am incredibly competitive. I have had some wonderful highs and big lows in my career and last November [when he lost the captaincy] was one of the latter. It did not teach me anything about myself that I did not know. The captaincy meant the world to me, but it is only ever a seat that you keep warm for someone else.

Life serves up other priorities, but playing rugby is the main thing. You always have a fear you are going to be dropped, but I was never going to walk away; playing for your country is a privilege. I have always had a professional relationship with Warren and will continue to do so. What has happened in the past has gone and I am just looking forward. It is not a case of right or wrong but what works for you. The events of last autumn will not have any impact on the World Cup. It is all about the future and when I heard that I was in the squad for New Zealand my reaction was one of pure delight. It was a huge day in my house when the 30 names were announced.'

Jones was a central figure in 2008 and a measure of how Wales had progressed was that injuries no longer made them vulnerable. When Gatland announced his team to face Ireland, Rhys Gill replaced Gethin Jenkins at prop. His only previous cap had come as a replacement against Ireland in 2010, but he had established himself in the front row of the English Premiership champions Saracens. Another player returning after a long absence was the second row Ian Evans. He had made his debut on the 2006 tour to Argentina and made four appearances under Gatland in the 2008 Six Nations. He suffered a knee injury playing against New Zealand the following November and it was more than two years before he added to his sixteen caps. By the end of the 2012 Six Nations, he had featured in nine matches in the tournament and had not once finished on the losing side. 'It was all about remaining positive during the tough times,' he said. 'I had a few setbacks along the way, but I knew I had to remain positive. I guess I have learned that nothing is guaranteed: you never know what is around the corner.'

The one match Evans had missed four years before had been against Ireland at Croke Park. The following year, when Ireland arrived in Cardiff needing victory to secure the grand slam, Gatland had raised the temperature by remarking that the team his players most disliked playing against was the Irish. He made his remarks after announcing his team: his habit then was to speak to a huddle of newspaper reporters away from the cameras and microphones so that what he said would not be reported until the following day. He sometimes used the occasion to make an incendiary remark that he knew would start a media fire, but in this instance it blew back into his face. Ireland were sure to have a significant number of players in the Lions squad for the tour to South Africa later that year and, as the forwards coach, Gatland had to work with them. The captain turned out to be Ireland's Paul O'Connell, and Gatland headed off any discontent on the other side of the Irish Sea by making an apology, pointing out that he had not meant his remarks to be taken in a personal context: he had been trying to highlight the rivalry between the two countries that the then Magners League had generated, adding an extra twist to Six Nations encounters.

Gatland has since stopped doing the huddles, and the only time he addresses the media in the week of a match is when he announces the team. His theme before the opening match in the 2012 competition was that Ireland would be anxious to avenge the World Cup quarter-final defeat to Wales. Ireland had been billed as potential winners of the tournament after they not just defeated but took apart Australia at forward in the group match between the sides at Eden Park. It was one of the biggest shocks in World Cup history: only Wales of the Celtic nations had defeated one of the major southern hemisphere nations in the World Cup, Australia back in 1987 when the two teams met in the third-place play-off. England had been the only home union to achieve the feat in a pool match, against South Africa in 2003, and Ireland's success meant that one path to the final would be an all Six Nations affair and the other would be contested by the four teams that would take part in the tournament that in 2012 would succeed the Tri-Nations: New Zealand, Australia, South Africa and Argentina. Wales had expected, after losing their opening group match to South Africa, to be facing the Wallabies in the quarter-final, and their bitter disappointment at losing to the Springboks by a point in their opening pool match was assuaged: it was South Africa who faced Australia in the last eight the day after Wales had beaten Ireland.

Ireland had not forgotten the manner of their defeat in Cardiff in March 2011. Wales's 19–13 victory was their only one at the Millennium Stadium that season. The difference between the sides was a converted try scored by the scrum-half Mike Phillips in the second half. It came from a quick throw taken by the hooker Matthew Rees after Jonathan Sexton, who had only just replaced Ronan O'Gara, kicked the ball into touch on the full. Ireland had not been expecting a quick lineout because the ball Sexton had kicked over the touchline had not only been touched by someone in the crowd but it had been thrown to a Wales player who did not take the throw and who still had it in his hands when the lineout was taken, three reasons for a referee under the laws not to allow a quick lineout to stand, but a different ball had been handed to Rees by a ball-boy a few metres away from the referee, Jonathan Kaplan, another breach of the laws. When Phillips crossed in the corner, Irish players protested immediately, led by their captain, Brian O'Driscoll. They were waved away as Kaplan asked the touch judge, Peter Allan, whether the ball that had been used by Rees was the one that had been kicked by Sexton. When he received the answer yes, he awarded the try. While Allan was in the wrong, Kaplan still did not have sufficient reason to signal for a try. He should also have asked whether anyone other than Rees had handled the ball. Ireland protested afterwards and received an apology from Allan, but the result stood and Wales had secured their first victory in the Six Nations over a country other than Italy or Scotland for more than two years.

'Ireland are incredibly dangerous when they talk about payback,' said Gatland. 'They will be disappointed by the way they played against us in the quarter-final. I think tactically we got a lot of things right that day and our loose forwards were outstanding. Rhys Priestland was very good on the day and it was an excellent performance, which is why they are talking about revenge. Their provinces are doing well in the Heineken Cup, and it is going to be a tough ask for us. You only have to look at the way Ireland played at the end of last year's Six Nations when England came to Dublin looking for the grand slam. They came up against a very motivated team and lost. We have three home games out of the next four to follow, but we cannot look beyond Sunday. If we win, it sets us up for a potentially successful championship. We tried to creep in under the radar in the World Cup. We knew we were in great shape physically and, although no one was talking about us, we were quietly confident. There is now a huge amount of expectation on us to do well and people are talking us up a bit. We have to have the confidence and belief that we can do well in this tournament, and the challenge for us is to accept that as a team. It hasn't always sat well with us. I think my experience with Welsh teams is that there are two times when we are at our most dangerous – when we have our backs to the wall and when we are playing with confidence.

'I thought it was the latter case in the World Cup when we showed self-belief and confidence; that's why we had such a good tournament.'

Tipping Point

Wales's quarter-final victory over Ireland had been a tactical triumph. Ireland had dragged Australia into a scrummaging and mauling contest, using their power up front and strength in the back row to dictate the game. Wales resolved to make sure the ball was on the floor in the quarter-final: that meant keeping off-loads to a minimum, reducing the opportunities for Ireland to keep a ball-carrier upright and get the put-in to a scrum should Wales fail to get the ball out of the subsequent maul, and going low to make tackles, bringing ball-carriers to ground immediately and preventing Ireland from generating any drives. A telling statistic from the match was that Ireland's back rowers carried the ball on 44 occasions for a total of 44 metres, meaning they were generally felled behind the gainline. Sean O'Brien alone had covered an average of nearly four metres on the twelve occasions he took on Australia's defence. Gatland wrong-footed Ireland from the outset: one of their tactics when they won in Cardiff in 2009 had been to send cross-kicks for the wing Tommy Bowe to contest against his shorter Ospreys colleague Shane Williams, a tactic that yielded one of their tries. Williams had been named on the left wing, opposite Bowe, in Wellington, but Gatland never had any intention of playing him there. Bowe found himself confronting the much taller North while Williams was up against a player barely taller than him, Keith Earls. Ireland seemed flummoxed from the start. The conditions appeared to suit them, with Wellington wet and very windy, and they had chosen O'Gara at outside-half, but after Williams had scored an early try, Ireland twice turned down the chance of a kickable penalty to put the ball into touch. They were shunted backwards each time and although they drew level early in the second half with a try from Earls, they finished well beaten. Having outfought Australia, they were out-thought by Wales.

And so talk of revenge swirled in the Dublin air on the Sunday of the game. Ireland were without their captain and talisman Brian O'Driscoll, who was to miss the entire Six Nations because of a shoulder injury. Earls was chosen as his replacement at outside-centre, but he pulled out before the match for family reasons and was replaced by Fergus McFadden. O'Driscoll had made his reputation for the danger he posed with the ball in hand, but he was just as threatening in defence, one of the most effective counter-ruckers in the game. Wales wanted a high ball-in-play time: they calculated that if it were in play for 37 minutes or less, the odds would be on an Ireland victory; if they got it to 40 minutes or more, the chances were that Wales would prevail. Not that the bookmakers fancied Wales. The Betting Directory website reported on the morning of the match that the odds on an Ireland victory were an ungenerous 2/5 while Wales were 2/1. 'Recent history strongly suggests an Ireland win,' punters were told, 'possibly with a winning margin of between 16 and 20 points. Wales can argue in their favour that they have won the last two encounters between the sides, although this carries little weight when they are under-strength and playing in front of a sell-out, partisan Irish crowd.'

Wales were without five of the side that had started the World Cup quarter-final: Cuthbert for the retired Williams was the only change behind, but the four changes at forward meant that Wales had two players who had not been part of the squad in New Zealand, Gill and Evans. Ireland's three changes were all behind the scrum: O'Driscoll and Earls were unavailable and Jonathan Sexton, who had been on the bench in Wellington, swapped places with O'Gara.

Wales, as they had done in Wellington, started strongly in what was Gatland's 50th match in charge and the hooker Huw Bennett's 50th cap. Davies's try put them 5–3 ahead after Sexton had kicked an early penalty, but Priestland hit the post with the conversion from out wide. He had been given the kicking duties because he had had the responsibility during the World Cup and scored twenty-nine points in five matches. Leigh Halfpenny had been used as the long-range kicker, but since returning from New Zealand he had become Cardiff Blues' first-choice goal-kicker ahead of the Scotland outside-half Dan Parks and had been notably successful. 'Leigh has a fantastic work ethic and we have pushed him to be first choice at the Blues,' said the Wales kicking coach Neil Jenkins before the team announcement. 'He has been doing that in the last month and that is an added bonus for us. He is putting his hand up and is applying pressure on the other kickers. We will decide who will take the kicks when the time is right. We are lucky to have so many top-quality kickers in the squad. We had a bad day in the World Cup semi-final and stuff happens. You do not get out of bed every morning and have a good day. We have moved on.'

Priestland hit a post again after 20 minutes when Wales had been awarded a penalty, but this time the kick was from almost in front. Wales were dominating possession and territory but not turning their position into points. They lost three of their own lineout throws and went into the interval five points behind. After Sexton had missed a penalty, Ireland worked space for their captain Rory Best to score. Sexton's conversion made it 10–5 to the hosts at the break and a concern for Wales was the ball-in-play time: at 16 minutes, it was some way short of what they felt they needed it to be to win, and when they returned for the second half they were without their captain, Warburton, who had suffered a dead leg, and Cuthbert. James Hook took over at full-back with Halfpenny moving to the wing, while Justin Tipuric, who had won two caps as a replacement in 2011, came on for Warburton, whose absence meant that Wales were down to three of the pack that had started the quarter-final. Ireland then quickly extended their lead after Rhys Gill had been penalised at a ruck and Sexton accepted the three points on offer.

When Priestland missed his third kick of the afternoon, the eight points squandered equalling the difference between the sides, his rueful look suggested it would be one of those days, but O'Brien was penalised shortly afterwards, and Halfpenny took aim at the posts and made the score 13–8. Two minutes later, Wales were in the lead after a try that was made by North's pace, power and dexterity. The gameplan had been, as in Wellington, not to off-load, but when Tipuric won the ball at the back of a lineout, North came from deep into the midfield and ran at McFadden. The centre could do no more than slow down the wing and wait for help to arrive but North, appreciating that the focus was on him, slipped a pass out of the back of his hand to Jonathan Davies on his outside and the midfielder ran 30 metres for his second try of the afternoon. Halfpenny's conversion put Wales back in front with 24 minutes to go.

Ireland responded in what was becoming an increasingly open game. Sexton kicked his third penalty on the hour and the lead changed hands for the fourth time. The final quarter was when Wales had asserted themselves in the World Cup, but after 65 minutes they found themselves down to 14 men. The second row Bradley Davies, who had lost his place in the starting line-up to Charteris during the World Cup, was sent to the sin-bin for dropping his opposite number, Donnacha Ryan, to the ground head first. It was not a tip tackle because the pair had been tussling off the ball: Davies had taken exception to the way Ryan had charged into the prop Adam Jones at a ruck; it was similar to the action of the South Africa second row Bakkies Botha on Jones in the second Test against the

2009 Lions. Jones had then suffered a shoulder injury that had ruled him out of the rest of the tour and Botha, much to the disgust of the Springboks, was banned after being cited. Davies's action was not seen by the referee, Wayne Barnes, who had to rely on the touch judge David Pearson for advice. Warburton had been sent off 19 minutes into the World Cup semi-final against France for tip-tackling the wing Vincent Clerc: he had not been the first player to commit the offence in the tournament, but whereas previous culprits had been shown a yellow card and been suspended after being cited, the Wales captain was a victim of a crackdown on the offence by the International Rugby Board, which had reminded referees that it was a red card offence and that the intent of a player made no difference because of the potentially dangerous nature of the act. Warburton had let go of Clerc, not dumped him head-first on the ground, but it made no difference and the referee in the semi-final, Alain Rolland, needed no reminding from the IRB. The previous January, he had sent off the Toulouse centre Florian Fritz for tip-tackling Tom Varndell during the Heineken Cup group match at Wasps. Rolland assumed the popularity in Wales of Roger Quittenton, the English referee who had awarded the All Blacks a match-winning penalty in Cardiff one minute from time after the second row Andy Haden, in a choreographed move, had jumped out of a lineout as if he had been shoved, but the Irishman had been given no room for discretion; like the players, he was bidding to be involved in a World Cup final and the zeitgeist of the time demanded that he show a red card, no matter the occasion.

Davies should have been sent off for an act of foul play, as Gatland, who let the second row know exactly what he thought after the match, admitted in the post-match media conference. Davies was subsequently cited and banned for twelve weeks, which was reduced by five weeks because of mitigating factors, such as his admission of guilt, his contrition and his previously good disciplinary record. He would play no part in the rest of the Six Nations. His suspension was an admission that Pearson had got it wrong, but Ireland took advantage of Davies's absence to score their second try of the match and extend their lead to six points. O'Connell stole another of Wales's lineout throws and Ireland switched play to expose a defence that was a man short, Sexton and Rob Kearney combining for Bowe to score the first of his five tries in the tournament. Sexton missed the conversion from wide out on the right and then botched a penalty from inside his own half. Wales were struggling to obtain possession but Ireland started to kick the ball away rather than keep it in hand. Wales were awarded a penalty, which Priestland kicked to touch. This time the lineout was secure and Wales moved the ball for Roberts and Davies to send in North. Halfpenny's conversion attempt to put Wales ahead was from the left-hand touchline and the ball drifted wide of the right-hand upright. There were four minutes left and Wales were trailing by a point. They needed to secure the restart and they did through Ryan Jones, although he was nearly barged off the ball by Toby Faletau. They slowly and patiently worked their way up field, making metres at a time but retaining possession. They had made their way towards the Ireland 22 when Evans was tackled above the horizontal by the Ireland flanker Stephen Ferris. Barnes awarded a penalty and sent Ferris to the sin-bin, decisions that angered Ireland. Halfpenny, as he had against France in the semi-final, had the chance to win the match.

'I said to myself after the semi-final that the next time I had a kick to win a game, I would nail it,' said Halfpenny afterwards. 'I did not think it would come so soon but it was what I had been waiting for. I was chuffed when the penalty was awarded, even if my heart was soon pounding as I started to feel the pressure of the moment. A supporter approached me after the match and asked whether the booing of the crowd had put me off. I had not noticed it, wrapped up as I was in my ritual. I blocked everything out and treated the kick as if it were any other. I knew it was my moment and I had to put myself back on the field in Gorseinon.' The kick was considerably shorter than the one he had lined up in the semi-final, 35 metres compared to almost 50, and it was slightly to the right of the posts. It was a kick Halfpenny would have landed virtually every time in practice, but this was a test of nerve rather than ability. He never looked like missing. 'It was a great feeling when it went over because it had been the hardest kick I had taken in my career,' he said. 'Thirty-odd metres seems an awfully long way away when you are in a position to seal a Six Nations game. It was not a case of making up for the semi-final but getting us off to a winning start in the Six Nations and keeping alive our aim of winning the grand slam. What we needed to show was that our experiences in the World Cup had made us stronger and I think we did.'

It was only the fifth time Wales had started a Six Nations campaign with a victory but Gatland admitted to being relieved rather than satisfied by the 23–21 success. 'We were reasonably lucky,' he said. 'I thought we were only at about 70 per cent of what we were capable of. We got out of jail, but we have won our first game of the tournament away from home. A displeasing aspect was the lack of discipline with the yellow card: I have seen a replay of the incident and it was not fantastic. We potentially have to prepare for the worst with a citing, but to come back at a place like this with 14 men shows great character. The victory will give us massive confidence and we are dangerous when we have that. At the same time, we know there is a lot we have to improve on. We should have not put so much pressure on Rhys by giving him the goal-kicking duty. He had been out injured for a while, but he was excellent in the second half.'

The match statistics were largely in Wales's favour. They enjoyed 58 per cent of the territory and 57 per cent of the possession. They passed the ball 177 times to Ireland's 128 and made 433 metres with the ball in hand compared to Ireland's 332. There were only two mauls in the game compared to 212 rucks, and while Wales lost four of their 14 lineouts their tactic of not kicking to touch unless there was no option, not wanting to put themselves in a position of having to defend driving mauls, meant that the bulk of Ireland's five throws came from penalties they had been awarded. Ireland also felt the impact of Wales's physical back division, missing 14 tackles.

The Wales scrum-half Mike Phillips was named the man of the match but felt the award should have gone to North. 'I gave everything and worked hard for the team,' he said, 'but I do not think I deserved to be man of the match. So many boys played well and a couple of touches by George were world-class. It is superb to have someone like him around. He's a great bloke as well. He works hard on his game and he has tremendous talent. He's got total star quality, which not many players have, but he is a totally down-to-earth guy, not big-headed in any way. He can just turn games. What is significant about this result is the way we won: I have been part of teams that have lost in the last few minutes, and while there are aspects of our game we want to improve on, we are a side that gets better the longer a competition goes on. I don't think that many people gave us much hope of beating Ireland, but we believed. We finished the game strongly and we nailed the final minutes.'

The last time Wales had started a championship campaign with a victory over Ireland had been 20 years before in 1992, another year following a World Cup. Neil Jenkins kicked three penalties in a 16–15 success. 'This was a huge performance,' he said after the 2012 victory in Dublin. 'It was one of our best results as a coaching team and showed how the boys play for the jersey and for the team. That is what it is all about at the end of the day: you want to play for your region but the reality is you want to play for Wales and win for Wales. That has been evident since Gats has been here. We have pushed that forward as coaches and the players put their bodies on the line; that is what it is all about.'

The match at the Aviva Stadium had been the last held on the opening weekend. Wales suddenly found themselves more fancied for the title after France's patchy victory over Italy in Paris and England's hard-fought victory over Scotland at Murrayfield, their first at the ground since 2004. France had taken advantage of some feeble tackling to record the biggest victory of the round, but the way Wales used the ball in Dublin, moving it wide or taking it up as required, together with the skill shown by their imposing back division, showed two things: first, that they were building on the World Cup and, second, that they were not missing Shane Williams as much as had been feared. The latter point could be taken further: Wales had got themselves into a position where they were able to cope with the loss of players with the minimum of disruption and no discernible dip in performance, something they had not been able to do in 2009 and 2010. Davies's impending suspension meant they would be without their leading three second rows against Scotland the following Sunday and it turned out that they would also be missing Warburton and Tipuric, leaving Gatland to find another open-side flanker. When he had arrived in Wales at the end of 2007, his priority had been to persuade Martyn Williams, the wing forward who had announced his retirement from international rugby at the end of that year's World Cup, to make himself available again. Gatland succeeded, as he had to because of the lack of alternatives, but by the beginning of 2012 the only position that was low on stock was tight-head prop, where Adam Jones had no rivals. Wales played with depth and they had depth.

3

Smart Alex

You'll never win anything with kids.

Alan Hansen

THE ONE CERTAINTY ABOUT WALES'S MATCH AGAINST
Scotland on the second Sunday in the 2012 Six Nations
was that there would be no headlines the following day
about a player taking a golf buggy along the M4 in search
of an early breakfast or becoming embroiled in trouble in
a club or bar in the centre of Cardiff. It had been different
the last time the Scots had been in Cardiff two years before.
Wales had won 31–24 with a burst of seventeen points in
the final three minutes in one of the most remarkable
finishes seen at the Millennium Stadium. Scotland had
looked on course for their first away victory in the
championship for four years and their first at the
Millennium Stadium since 2004, having surprised Wales
with their sense of adventure. The 2008 grand slam was a
fading memory for Wales, who had lost three of their
previous four games in the Six Nations, a five-point victory
over Italy in Rome interrupting defeats to France, Ireland
and England. They were outplayed for long periods in a
match that marked the end of the career of the Scotland
wing Thom Evans, who suffered a serious neck injury after

a tackle, but, in a sign of what was to come, they prevailed at the end.

Scotland had their hooker Scott Lawson in the sin-bin when Leigh Halfpenny scored a try under the posts for Stephen Jones to convert and close the deficit to three points. Wales were then awarded a penalty after the referee sent Phil Godman to the sin-bin for tripping Lee Byrne, leaving Scotland two men down. The Wales captain, Ryan Jones, pondered whether to take the three points and tie the scores. After being told by the referee George Clancy that there would be time for one more play, he asked Stephen Jones to take the kick and the outside-half duly converted it. Scotland's coach, Andy Robinson, already infuriated that a rare victory had turned into a draw, tried to get a message to his players that the kick-off should be put directly into touch because Wales would not have time to take a lineout. The players had been told by Clancy that there were nine seconds left and Mike Blair, who took the kick-off with Godman in the sin-bin and Dan Parks having been replaced, kept the ball in play. Wales took possession and set out to exploit their two-man advantage: a Stephen Jones cross-kick for Byrne alarmed the crowd, but the full-back made the catch and when the second row Bradley Davies charged towards the Scotland line there was a clear overlap. Wales kept their nerve and Shane Williams completed the comeback with a try under the posts. 'It was the most amazing match I have been involved in as a coach or player,' said Warren Gatland, not someone who is given to exaggeration. Robinson said his side had committed suicide but accused Byrne of getting Godman sent to the sin-bin by feigning contact. 'I jumped up to try to get the ball,' said Godman. 'There was no malice at all. He milked it. I did not stick my foot out and trip him; he put himself into my body.' Byrne denied the charge, saying: 'The video evidence will show it was a trip. I kicked the ball through and Phil left his foot there. If he is going to do that, he has to expect to be penalised. It was the referee's call about the yellow card, but I had no doubt it was deserving of a penalty.'

Wales were on a high and, as they had a rest weekend coming up, the players were allowed to celebrate. The Wales management had reinforced the squad's code of conduct relating to alcohol the previous year after four players were involved in an incident in a Cardiff bar that led to the police being called out. Wales had beaten England at the Millennium Stadium the previous day but there was no basking in that success because the headlines the following week concentrated on the behaviour of four players, Gavin Henson, Andy Powell, Rhys Thomas and Jonathan Thomas. Gatland and the Wales team manager Alan Phillips conducted an investigation and issued a rebuke to the four, each of whom admitted to 'varying degrees of regrettable conduct'. 'They have all been warned that their involvement in events will be taken into account in future if they are party to any incidents where misconduct is apparent by any squad member,' said the Welsh Rugby Union in a statement. Henson, who newspaper reports described as having been 'particularly rowdy' during the bar crawl, apologised after claims that he had been abusive to customers. The previous season, Henson had also been involved in an incident on a train on his way back from London after Ospreys had beaten Harlequins that saw him hit with a charge of disorderly behaviour that was subsequently dropped. Because he lived at the time with the singer Charlotte Church, Henson was a magnet for popular newspapers and magazines.

Gatland was furious that the achievement of a third successive victory over England in the Six Nations had been overshadowed by players being out on the town at a time they were expected to be at home. 'What happened was not acceptable,' said Alan Phillips. 'We felt let down but everyone knows where they stand now and it is time to move on. If there is a repeat of this, we will not be so charitable. These are tough times with people losing their jobs and it's very important that we conduct ourselves properly. We had managed things well on Saturday night as a team. We didn't stop anyone having a few beers in a controlled environment to celebrate the win because there were two weeks to the next game. There was no need for anyone to be out on Sunday. We should have turned up on Wednesday after a few days off really bouncing and happy after a very good win but this has just made life difficult. What happened on Sunday will not impact on selection. We are dealing with young people aged between 20 and 30, and some of them react to disappointment in different ways. They need to have a blowout occasionally but there has to be a time and a place for it. None of the players involved tried to hide away from what had happened. They did not run away and make excuses but fronted up. Given the pressures they are under, they will slip up occasionally.'

It was Phillips who prompted a sea change in the way the management and the players dealt with the issue of alcohol. He was suspended from the squad in the summer of 2011 after pictures of him being wrestled to the ground by bouncers outside a burger bar in the centre of Cardiff in the early hours of a Tuesday morning and being held until police arrived were posted on the Internet. It was an example of how the media world had changed for players: in days past, they had been able to rely on the discretion of reporters to keep incidents in bars or on the street out of the newspapers, but the advent of mobile phones with cameras and social media such as Facebook and Twitter meant that every citizen was a potential journalist. The wall of trust that had existed between players and reporters had fallen with the end of amateurism: the two groups no longer socialised and there was a concern in rugby circles that reporting had become obsessed with individuals at the expense of the game itself, with Henson an obvious case in point.

Phillips was not charged after the burger-bar incident, merely taken away from the area in a police van. His humiliation lay in the incident instantly being relayed around the world, and the WRU took immediate action. 'The Wales management team will take time to consider circumstances surrounding recent allegations about the player's behaviour in public whilst on an agreed holiday period from pre-Rugby World Cup training,' said the WRU in a statement. 'Phillips has been told not to report to WRU headquarters at the National Centre of Excellence this Monday – the preordained start date of his personal training regime – and will remain outside of the squad until further notice. The suspension has been approved by Wales head coach Warren Gatland and agreed by the senior squad management team. The WRU has not been alerted of any criminal action and the suspension is based on its own behaviour protocols.' The Union's chief executive, Roger Lewis, went further when he said: 'Mike Phillips is an exceptional player, but there is irrefutable evidence of a prima facie nature that he was engaged in behaviour that falls below the standards we set. It is vitally important that we send out a clear and unambiguous message to one and all concerning our views on matters of this sort. That message must be heard clearly by all players, coaches, administrators, volunteers, supporters and, of course, the parents and guardians of any child attracted to take part in the national sport of Wales. By taking decisive action now we are emphasising that this sort of incident is highly unusual in that the majority of people involved in Welsh rugby help us maintain the proud record we have for fair play and off-the-field courtesy. Our senior national squad players are highly visible because of the profile that accompanies the success of our national sport and it is made clear to them that they are the ambassadors we rely on to foster and sustain our image. An incredible amount of hard work is currently taking place as our players prepare for the Rugby World Cup in New Zealand and that effort must be recognised and supported by all involved. I am making my views public at this time because, as the nation anticipates our involvement in the Rugby World Cup there is no room for any ambiguity in our reasoning. Rugby is part of the culture of our nation and we must do all in our power to ensure that the game remains a sport that everyone in Wales can be rightly proud of.'

Phillips's suspension lasted ten days. Gatland only allowed him back into the squad after being given assurances by the player that he would get professional help to address behavioural issues. He had that month signed for Bayonne after being released from his contract by Ospreys and admitted that the burger-bar incident had left him feeling humiliated. 'This is the most embarrassing thing that has happened to me in my career,' he said. 'I am ashamed to have let myself get into this kind of situation and I am determined to put things right. As a player I'm really passionate and never back down. I know I can't allow that part of my character to come to the surface off the rugby pitch. I have realised I have an issue with the way in which I deal with, and have dealt with, the pressures of my current environment and have sought, and will continue to seek, help and advice in relation to that issue.'

The last player to have been suspended by Gatland was the number 8 Andy Powell after the 2010 match against Scotland. Powell had returned to the team's hotel in the early hours of Sunday morning but a few hours later was spotted driving down the M4, which was little more than a mile from where the team was based, heading eastwards towards the services in a golf buggy he had commandeered from the hotel. Powell was to have a bit-part role in the 2012 grand slam, coming on as a replacement in the final six minutes against Scotland, but his international career looked over when he was arrested by police at the service station where he had gone in search of breakfast at 5.40 a.m. He was charged with driving a mechanically propelled vehicle while unfit through drink and he was immediately thrown out of the Wales squad. 'We take matters of player conduct extremely seriously and have been happy with the professionalism and discipline of this squad in general terms,' said Alan Phillips. 'Andy knows he has misbehaved and is apologetic but he also knows that he must take responsibility for his own actions and accept the repercussions. This kind of behaviour cannot be tolerated in a professional, elite sporting environment and we have acted quickly and incisively to leave no ambiguity over the dim view we take of this situation. The player has made his private apologies to the Welsh management team as well as apologising in a public statement and we have also asked him to apologise to the Vale Resort Hotel before leaving the squad.'

Powell had won 14 Wales caps. Gatland caused surprise when he named the then 27-year-old forward in the side to face South Africa in November 2008. Powell's career had taken him from Newport, Béziers and Leicester to the Scarlets and Cardiff Blues. He never settled for long but he made such an impact in his first season with Wales as a ball-carrying number 8 that he was chosen for the Lions tour to South Africa. Gatland also liked the way

Powell lightened the mood in the squad by cracking jokes and winding others up, but it was to be another nine months before Powell represented his country again. He was given a 15-month driving ban when he appeared before Cardiff magistrates in March 2010 and admitted the charge of driving while unfit through drink. He was also fined £1,000, with £85 costs, and ordered to pay a £15 victim surcharge. The court heard that Powell had told the police after he had been apprehended: 'I am a professional rugby player. What have I done? I took the buggy as a prank but decided to attend the services for some munchies with friends. I am an idiot, I know.' Powell's lawyer, Conrad Gadd, said in mitigation: 'It had been a great day for Wales and the Welsh rugby team. They snatched victory in the final minutes and at the final whistle the euphoria began. Beer is a staple of any rugby side and here there was more than a few pints of beer. Mr Powell was out in the early hours of the morning and by 5.30 a.m. he and a colleague were hungry. He does not know if he will be readmitted [to the Wales squad]. He is in limbo. This isn't bad driving here. It is foolhardy driving.'

A few months later, Powell was released by Cardiff Blues and joined Wasps, where the Wales defence coach Shaun Edwards was the head coach. He failed to last the season, leaving the club by mutual consent after he became involved in a brawl with football supporters in a pub in the west of London. He was hit by a bar stool and lost consciousness. He joined Sale a few months later and was part of Wales's World Cup squad, although he did not start a game in New Zealand.

Gadd's assertion that beer was the staple of any rugby side did not apply to Wales from the 2011 World Cup onwards. The game had changed, anyway, in the professional era. When a side from the British Isles toured

South Africa in 1896, it was decided that the habit of knocking back large volumes of alcohol on the morning of a match was having an adverse effect on performance and a crackdown was announced: players would be limited to no more than four tumblers of champagne each before a game. Graham Price, the prop who played for Wales between 1975 and 1983, believes a problem for players in the modern game is that they have a lower tolerance threshold to alcohol than their amateur predecessors. 'We used to play twice a week and that meant two drinking sessions,' he said. 'We were used to beer but the players today go for long periods on the wagon. They are far more abstemious than we were.' During the 2011 World Cup, after Wales had reached the semi-finals, Alan Phillips recalled the time that they had reached that stage, back in 1987, when he was in the squad as a hooker. 'We beat England in the quarter-final and we were given two days off,' he said. 'We got so wrecked on the first day that Clive Rowlands [the then manager] went mad and cancelled the next day off, making us come in for training. In those days, we drank beer, which you could sweat off in training, but there is a lot more variety in pubs now. What we have in the Wales squad now is a group of hardworking players who are prepared to make sacrifices. Everything they do is geared to being successful on the rugby field and they are a credit to the nation.'

Fifteen of the players in Wales's 2011 thirty-five-strong World Cup squad were twenty-three or younger. They had come through the academy system run by the WRU, a contrast to the route taken to the top by the prop Adam Jones, one of three players in 2012 to achieve the grand slam for a third time. 'When I was in youth teams, you would easily have ten or fifteen beers after a game,' he said. 'What we are getting in the Wales squad now are some freakishly talented youngsters. I remember when we were going for the grand slam in 2005 I did not have much of an idea how to handle the pressure. The academy system means that the youngsters now take it all in their stride. Nothing fazes them.'

While England were making the headlines in the New Zealand World Cup for the wrong reasons, with alcohol at the heart of the negative publicity, Wales were praised for their restraint. When Wales played the Barbarians in June 2011, Gatland made Sam Warburton the captain in the absence of Matthew Rees. The flanker was then 22 and had only that season replaced the veteran Martyn Williams on the open-side. When Rees had to pull out of the World Cup squad because he needed an operation on his neck, Gatland had no hesitation in giving Warburton the captaincy even though there were several more experienced players in the squad. It was not an appointment made with the future in mind because the World Cup was about the there and then: Gatland felt that Wales would benefit from the young players setting the example to their elders rather than the other way around. England went down the same route, but only after the tournament.

Much was made during the World Cup about how Wales had become teetotal. When the squad gathered before the tournament, they set up a dry and a wet board. 'Everyone started off dry and if you had a drink you moved yourself over to the wet board,' said Warburton during the tournament. 'It was an honesty call. I could count on one hand how many times I've had a drink here. After a game, players will be allowed to have maybe a bottle or two, those who feel they need to, because for some it helps them relax, but there is no binge-drinking going on at all. A while ago, players would have gone out after almost every game, but I think you have got to look at the bigger picture: there was no point in working so hard all summer just to drink at the pool stage. There were incidents in the Six Nations a couple of years ago but during this year's tournament we would be on the bus going back from a game and no one would go into Cardiff. It would be back to the hotel, a couple of drinks if you wanted and then in bed by midnight. That has been the way forward this year. In Cardiff now, you are such easy targets if you go out as a squad; it's too easy for negative things to happen. We have a fines committee here for things like any drinking when people shouldn't, putting things on social network sites they shouldn't, or even wearing the wrong colour socks. When the World Cup is over, then the players might have a well-earned drink after five months of pretty much being dry.'

What Gatland had insisted on during the World Cup was that the Wales players behaved responsibly. They were not banned from having the occasional beer, but they were encouraged to relax within the confines of the team hotel. When they did venture out into a town or city centre, they were given a 1 a.m. curfew. 'We have been painted out to be monks and that there has been an alcohol ban, but that is wrong,' said Gatland. 'There have been a couple of nights when the boys have had a beer in the hotel and we spoke to Sam and senior players about imposing a curfew when players go out. You cannot keep a lid on everything: if you play a game at night, there is a lot of adrenalin flowing. We have had our problems in the past but these guys are great ambassadors for Wales. What is important is that there has been a sea shift in terms of professionalism. A lot of hard work has gone in and the players knew when they arrived in New Zealand that they were in pretty good shape and that if they looked after themselves they could make an impact. And they have done that.'

The Welsh Grand Slam 2012

Wales had it right on and off the field. Their opponents in the second round of the 2012 Six Nations, in contrast, were in need of a victory. Scotland had failed to qualify for the quarter-finals of the World Cup for the first time, squeezed out by Argentina and England despite leading in the second half in both matches. They had failed to score a try in their final three pool matches, equalling a record set by Spain in 1999, and they had drawn another blank on the opening weekend of the Six Nations when they lost to England at Murrayfield for the first time since 2004 despite dominating territory and possession. Scotland had wasted three opportunities through players taking wrong options while England, despite barely mustering an attack, scored the game's only try when the outside-half Charlie Hodgson charged down his opposite number Dan Parks's attempted clearance. Parks, the Cardiff Blues 10, had intended to retire from international rugby after the World Cup but was persuaded to stay on because injuries had restricted the head coach Andy Robinson's options in the position. Robinson had named in his squad for the tournament Steven Shingler, the former Scarlets and Wales Under-20 stand-off who was playing for London Irish. Shingler qualified for Scotland through his mother but when he was named in their squad the WRU made an objection to the International Rugby Board, saying that he was ineligible.

Shingler had played for Wales in an Under-20 international against France in 2011. Wales had designated the Under-20s as their second team, which meant, under IRB regulations, that once a player appeared for them at that level he would not be able to represent another country if the team he played against also used the Under-20s as their second side. It led to confusion as some countries ran A sides, as France had done in 2010. That year, two players who appeared against the French for Wales in the Under-20 Six Nations, Matthew Jarvis and James Loxton, left Wales for Connacht. They were eligible to play for Ireland and when the WRU complained, it was ruled that as France did not use the Under-20s as their second side, the pair had not committed themselves to Wales. Shingler was not so fortunate and although he maintained he did not sign a form before the France international acknowledging that he was committing his international future to Wales, an IRB appeals committee subsequently decided that it did not matter. The panel was sufficiently perturbed at the system to point out that the Board's Council had the power to reverse the decision. It also recommended that a system that could see dual-qualified brothers appear in an Under-20 tournament and, depending on the teams they played against, finish it with one committed to the country he had played for while the other still had two options be reviewed. A Shingler did play in the Wales–Scotland fixture in the 2012 Six Nations; not Stephen but his older brother, Aaron, a flanker with the Scarlets who was drafted into the Wales team at the last moment after Warburton withdrew because the dead leg he had suffered the previous week had not cleared up.

Wales not only went into the Scotland game as firm favourites but they were being talked about as potential champions. 'It was a huge performance in Ireland,' said Neil Jenkins. 'We put a bit of pressure on ourselves and met fire with fire.' As kicking coach he had a conundrum before Sunday: who would take the goal-kicks, Halfpenny or Rhys Priestland? 'The goal-kicking did not start off too well, Rhys missing the kicks that he did, but that is the way it goes,' he reflected. 'I have been there myself as a player. Leigh's kick to win the match at the end was awesome. I looked at him just before he took it and said a few words. He could not have put it through the middle more and I was delighted for him. He works incredibly hard on his game and goes out kicking on Christmas Day. We will see who starts the goal-kicking at the end of the week. We know where Rhys is at: he is an outstanding player and he had a fantastic game on Sunday. I was very happy with his all-round kicking. I know he will be very frustrated with his goal-kicking, especially the one in front, which was a poor kick by his standards, but he hit the post twice. I was very impressed with his punting and restarts and he gives us so much in that area. Rhys has no issues. He kicked for us in the World Cup and against Australia and we felt he had the shirt and wanted to give him another chance.'

Priestland himself did not expect to be lining up the first kick against Scotland. 'I don't know yet what will happen because we haven't spoken about it,' he said. 'The way Leigh has kicked it's going to be hard for me to get it back off him. I have got to try to forget about what happened on the weekend and if I do get another opportunity I have to take it. If not, I'll just try to concentrate on every other aspect of the game. Let's just say it helped that we won on the weekend. I was disappointed and spoke to some of the coaches, saying it was a little bittersweet. I was not happy with the way I kicked, but I was delighted with the way we played in some areas of the game and, of course, that we got a win against such a strong Ireland team out there. I learnt a few years ago that you can't keep dwelling on things. You have to keep moving on. I used to beat myself up when things went wrong, worrying about what people thought and said. My coach at the Scarlets, Nigel Davies, told me not to worry and that those who criticised me could not do it themselves and to keep believing in myself. It took a while for me to be convinced, but if I do have a bad game now I try to forget about it, not go and hide. One off day in an international and people think someone else should be playing. I feel for Dan Parks: it was only two years ago when he had three man-of-the-matches in the Six Nations and then they went to Argentina and beat them. He's probably one of the best kickers out of hand, but Scotland haven't scored many tries and he's had a lot of criticism because of it. I only really played against him when he was with Glasgow. You used to go up there knowing what he was going to do, but you couldn't really stop him. He has won many games for Scotland and what has happened is a bit sad.'

Media attention was lavished on North, the boy mountain who had unsettled an Ireland defence that was regarded as one of the best in the international game: his try was his tenth in international rugby, and he was the youngest player to reach the landmark. He had been hired by the *Daily Mail* to provide a weekly column. In keeping with a player who was unlike any other, it was not the usual 700 words of continuous prose. It was broken up into segments, a snapshot of his week. 'The size of the landing in our hotel room in Dublin was bigger than my entire flat,' he wrote. 'I walked in and assumed it was a bedroom but it was just the cloakroom and I was thinking "what the hell?" We flew in on Friday and stayed at the Berkeley Court Hotel, which is unbelievable for a 19 year old. A comfy bed, soft pillows – it's a hundred miles from what we had in Poland. It was right next to the stadium and I could have jumped off the roof of the hotel and on to the pitch.' He also reflected on his meteoric rise. 'I try not to read anything about me because if you start reading too much hype then you'll get above yourself. Luckily, if I chirp up for a second the boys here or my dad at home will chop me down straight away. It goes the other way, too. A lot of people lost a lot of confidence in me at the start of the season and said I'd just had a lucky break with beginners' luck and all that.

It can get a bit too much when you're 19. Now I've just got to try to play well every week – and, I hope, for the next ten years.' He revealed he did not drink coffee on the day of a game. 'It would be like putting a sugar cube in a Coke can and shaking it. Aged 19 on game day with caffeine? I'd go nuts.'

Priestland, a colleague of North's at the Scarlets, remembered the first time he met the wing. 'He started training with the region before the start of last season. We were doing some gym training and this guy was so much stronger than anyone else in the squad. I asked him whether he had done much with his time off. He said he had had exams. I asked if they were university ones and he said no, A levels. He has not stopped surprising me since. I was behind George when he gave the off-load for Jonathan Davies's second try and could not believe what I saw. At the age of 19, he is a superstar of the game but he is someone who concentrates on the basics. He tries to get over the gainline, he runs hard and he has good support lines.'

Wales were strengthened by the return to fitness of Gethin Jenkins and Dan Lydiate, but neither was guaranteed an immediate return to the side because of the way their replacements, Rhys Gill and Ryan Jones, had performed in Dublin. Jones was a candidate to replace the suspended Bradley Davies with the second row receiving a seven-week suspension after being cited for foul play at the Aviva Stadium. 'We adapted well to the injuries we had,' said the Wales forwards coach, Robin McBryde, who after the tournament became the final member of Gatland's management team to sign a new contract that took him to the end of the 2015 World Cup. 'We will miss Bradley but Ryan is one of a number of options we have in the second row. Alun Wyn Jones looks as if he may return for Ospreys on the weekend and we are also monitoring Luke Charteris, who is a little bit behind Alun Wyn. Rhys was outstanding against Ireland, using good leg-drive to get over the gainline and he scrummaged well. He put a marker down and I don't think anyone has put so much pressure on Gethin. Scotland were strong in the set-pieces against England and a bit more composure and better decision-making would have taken them home. They will be wounded and we left it a bit late against them two years ago. They will throw everything at us because this is their opportunity to get their campaign going.'

Wales again named their side on the Friday. Warburton was included even though he had only taken a limited part in training throughout the week. Jenkins and Lydiate returned with Ryan Jones replacing Davies in the second row. There were only four survivors from the side that had started against Scotland in Cardiff two years before and only two of those were playing in the same positions: Jamie Roberts and Adam Jones. Halfpenny had been on the right wing in 2010 with Ryan Jones leading the side from number 8. There were nine changes from the team that took to the field against Scotland at Murrayfield in 2011. 'We felt Gethin's experience was important given that we had lost Bradley Davies and Ryan had to move to the second row,' said Gatland. 'We did not consider changing the back division. When you look at the statistics from Scotland's game against England you wonder how they lost. They had opportunities and they will be frustrated. I understand they want the roof to be closed and it sounds as if both sides will be positive. We underestimated them a bit two years ago and they took their opportunities, making us dig deep. We have to make sure we are on our mettle and improve on Dublin. It will be a tighter game than people think. Scotland are not a negative side: they have just struggled to score tries from the opportunities they create. They want to play rugby but at times, perhaps, they have lacked the X factor and we may have the slight edge over them in a couple of players. We will make some subtle changes from Ireland in attack and defence. We have got to be smart about how we use George North. Modern rugby is about using your big men as decoys at times. We spoke last week about keeping our depth and width and staying square. We are lucky enough to have some firepower behind and if you have big men running hard and straight over 80 minutes, challenging inside shoulders, at some stage a tackle will be missed.'

One aspect of Dublin that displeased Gatland was the yellow card received by Davies. Discipline, or the lack of it, had been a recurring theme for Wales since the 2008 grand slam. Six players had been sent to the sin-bin in the last six away matches in the Six Nations. 'I have asked the players to come back with a suggestion on what we need to do in the future to have a deterrent for yellow cards,' said Gatland. 'I am not talking about ones that are picked up unluckily, but we have had them in the past which have been unnecessary. Whatever I am saying is not working with some individuals. I have criticised players publicly in the past and then been criticised myself for having a go at them. I did suggest that a fine of £20,000 or £30,000 may be relevant but I don't think they were too keen on that! I then suggested doing a week of visits in primary schools and we will come up with something in the next few weeks that the squad is happy with. Bradley got caught up in the moment and reacted to Donnacha Ryan hitting Adam Jones. He knows he made a mistake and he has got to learn from it. Young men make mistakes. Some of our Valleys boys don't need to have that big macho image. His punishment is not just the seven weeks he will miss: it is also financial as he will lose match fees and win bonuses potentially. I hope to see a more composed player in the future.' It was not Wales, though, who were to see red over yellow cards come the day of the game.

Wales started the match in third place in the table. England were top after recording a second victory on the road, coming from behind to defeat Italy in the snow in Rome. France's match that night against Ireland had been postponed just before the kick-off because of a frozen pitch and rescheduled for the second fallow weekend in the tournament. It meant that when France visited the Millennium Stadium on the last weekend of the campaign, they would be playing their fourth match in as many weeks. The prospect of facing Les Bleus last up at home was tempting some to speculate about a grand slam: Wales had achieved the clean sweep with victory over France in 1950, 1952, 1971, 1976, 1978 and 2008, and only in the odd-numbered year had they done so in Paris. There had not been many years since the 1970s when Wales had to carry the burden of expectation and Halfpenny said the objective of the players at the start of the tournament had been clear.

'At the end of the day we want to be the best,' he said. 'That means winning every single game and achieving the grand slam. That is the aim for this tournament, nothing less. We are preparing for the Six Nations as we did the World Cup, another tournament we set out to win. We set high goals to bring the best out of us. We train as hard as possible and nothing less than our best will do. Everyone is ambitious, from the coaches to the players. Winning trophies is our goal and we believe we can achieve that. The loss against France in the World Cup semi-final has made us stronger. It made you go back and work harder: it gave you the drive to do better. We have strength in depth now, as we showed in Ireland, and that is the key to successful campaigns. We know there is a long way to go.'

Warburton was ruled out on the morning of the match after failing a fitness test. With Justin Tipuric also injured, Shingler, who had played cricket for Glamorgan, replaced Warburton; he was Wales's third open-side flanker in two matches. Shingler, who had qualified for England as well as Scotland before playing for Wales in Sevens because he was born in Hampshire, was not a specialist breakaway, operating on the blind-side for the Scarlets or even in the second row. He had finished the Heineken Cup in style, scoring an interception try against Castres after an 80-metre run that helped the region to victory and a place in the quarter-finals of the Amlin Challenge Cup. He had also been prominent in the home defeat against Northampton the previous week, aggressive and combative. His fellow uncapped colleague at the Scarlets, Lou Reed, was on the bench covering the second row and his perfect day was made when he came on as a replacement for Ryan Jones, who captained the side in the absence of Warburton, five minutes before the end.

Wales had only won their opening two matches in the Six Nations twice before, in 2005 and 2008, and on each occasion they had gone on to achieve the grand slam. Scotland not only had a poor record on the road in the tournament, they tended to win only one game in a campaign and it had been six years since they had done otherwise. One unusual statistic was that there was not one member of their match-day 22 who had kicked a goal in a Test match. Chris Paterson had retired from international rugby after the World Cup and Parks was no longer available. Parks's replacement at outside-half, Greig Laidlaw, a nephew of the 1980s Scotland and Lions scrum-half Roy Laidlaw, was making his first start in the Six Nations while the uncapped 19-year-old Stuart Hogg, who covered full-back, centre and stand-off, was on the bench, where the specialist 10 was a 30 year old who had yet to appear in a Test match, Duncan Weir.

Roger Lewis used his programme notes to appeal for unity in the Welsh game. A couple of weeks earlier, the Union had asked a firm of consultants to examine the financial state of the game in the country, covering both the four regions and the governing body, and there was concern that many more players would join Mike Phillips, James Hook and Lee Byrne in France.

He reminded readers that, following losses against England at the Millennium Stadium in the previous year's Six Nations and against the Barbarians in the summer of 2011, there had been rumblings about the state of Welsh rugby and calls for change in the WRU, but that in the wake of these defeats Wales had gone to the Rugby World Cup and had returned from New Zealand resurgent. Welsh rugby was, he emphasised, going through a period of strength, with victories on the pitch and success in the boardroom, too.

He warned, however, against complacency, pointing out that 'even on the warmest days, there are clouds somewhere in Wales'. He was referring, of course, to the difficult climate faced by Welsh regional rugby. While careful not to underplay the seriousness of the problems that needed to be addressed, Lewis stressed the importance of a positive, forward-looking attitude in tackling the challenges ahead. He assured supporters that all in Welsh rugby were pulling together to find solutions and strengthen the game as a whole, ending by stating: 'If we are inseparable, we will be insuperable.'

Wales did not look insuperable in the first half against Scotland but, as in the 1970s, they were adept at wearing sides down. They were not ahead at half-time once in their first three matches in the 2012 Six Nations and the side that won the grand slam in 1978 did so by winning margins of three, eight, four and nine points, scoring eight tries and conceding four. They made their highest score against Scotland, as they were to do 34 years later. The 1976 fixture against Scotland at the old National Stadium in Cardiff had been notable for something that had never happened before: the Wales players were banned from talking to newspaper reporters. John Billot, in his *History of Welsh International Rugby*, believed the move was a backlash from the Wales selectors who had been criticised for not only omitting Phil Bennett from the side that played England in the opening round but not including him as a replacement, effectively making him Wales's third-choice outside-half behind John Bevan and David Richards; injuries meant that Bennett took the field at Twickenham. 'The selectors pointed out that they imposed the sanction in players' interests to minimise the effects of modern investigative journalism and its consequent stress upon some players,' wrote Billot. 'The gag represented an infringement on players' freedom as individuals in an amateur game, though the system had become common practice and long been employed by the feudalists of Scotland, who nurture the distinction between superiors and vassals. The principal cause of stress to players was intensive coaching, the demands of the national squad and a rigorous club programme. Team preparation had been transformed from the free-and-easy run-out to near professional requirements.' The Wales squad then had two training sessions before a Six Nations match, on Sunday and Thursday, and only gathered at the team hotel on the Friday night. Professionalism demanded considerably more.

Scotland opened the scoring in the 2012 match, Laidlaw kicking his first points in international rugby after Wales had twice turned kickable penalties into lineouts. Wales started by running from their own 22, making 50 metres before Jonathan Davies knocked on. Wales's first lineout was overthrown and the Scots started to force mistakes, exerting pressure at the breakdown. Scotland had a lot of possession in the opening minutes, but Wales's line speed in defence forced them to play behind the gainline. Big hits abounded, Davies on Lee Jones, Rory Lamont on Priestland, and neither team was able to take play through multiple phases. Scotland used their forwards to cut down North, Ross Rennie ending a promising move from a lineout and Jim Hamilton bringing the wing to a juddering halt, but Wales then brought on their other wing, Alex Cuthbert, roughly the same weight, height and speed of North, and the Scots did not seem to have paid as much attention to him in their analysis. Scotland's first real thrust came from Rennie, but just as the flanker blew his side's best chance by holding on to the ball for too long after making a break, so he was caught with the ball after breaking into Wales's 22. It did give Scotland the position from which Laidlaw kicked his penalty after 22 minutes and the score prompted a reaction from Wales, another Cuthbert break and a penalty quickly taken by Phillips, leading to pressure being put on the Scottish line for the first time.

Wales drew level on 29 minutes when Halfpenny kicked a penalty after Alasdair Strokosch had impeded Phillips at a ruck and it was Halfpenny who ensured they did not go into the break behind with a copybook tackle on Rory Lamont after the full-back had taken advantage of North being treated for an ankle injury. Scotland took play through 20 phases before the prop Allan Jacobsen knocked on just short of the line. James Hook replaced North, moving to full-back with Halfpenny switching to the wing, but within 30 seconds of his arrival on the field, Romain Poite blew for half-time.

Huw Bennett did not reappear for the second half, replaced by Ken Owens, and a mistake by the Scotland scrum-half Chris Cusiter from Priestland's kick-off gave Wales an attacking lineout. Ian Evans secured the ball, Ryan Jones, Roberts and Faletau stormed the gainline and when the ball was moved right, Cuthbert moved into the midfield, took a short pass from Hook and stepped out of Laidlaw's tackle. Halfpenny's conversion gave Wales a 10–3 lead and then he kicked his second penalty of the match, which was awarded after Scotland had lost the ball in midfield and Jonathan Davies hacked it towards Scotland's 22. As he chased after his kick, he was taken out by the Scotland centre Nick de Luca, who was sent to the sin-bin, continuing the tradition of the visiting teams receiving yellow cards in the fixture: Wales had received two at Murrayfield in 2011, Bradley Davies and Byrne, matching Scotland's record in Cardiff the previous year. The Wales flanker Martyn Williams went to the sin-bin in 2009 and the Scotland second row Nathan Hines was given ten minutes off in 2008.

Wales's initial attempt to take advantage of their extra man failed when Shingler was turned over by Rennie and Laidlaw kicked his second penalty to make it 13–6 but Wales replied immediately, taking play from right to left and back again, sucking in defenders and creating the space out wide for Cuthbert to free Halfpenny, who had crossed over from his wing. Halfpenny's conversion made it 20–6 and when Wales went straight back onto the attack, Rory Lamont tackled Hook from an off-side position and he was shown the yellow card, leaving Scotland down to 13 men for 90 seconds. Ryan Jones told Priestland to kick for touch and although Scotland repelled the lineout drive, Wales were awarded a five-metre scrum. De Luca made a timely return to the field, but Wales attacked down the blind-side and Halfpenny skipped over for his second try, which he converted to make it 27–6 and leave Scotland with no way back. Wales eased up and, after Hogg had wrongly been denied a try, deemed to have knocked on a pass he caught, Laidlaw scored a try from a ruck on Wales's line and added the conversion.

It was the final score of the game, Halfpenny missing a 45-metre penalty to leave him on 22 points for the match, and Gatland for once emptied his bench. Gethin Jenkins was sent to the sin-bin three minutes from the end for not rolling away after a tackle, joking afterwards that he did not think the offence merited a £20,000 fine. 'It was touch and go in the first half, but we said at the interval that we just needed to look after the ball more and the chances would come,' said Lydiate, who was named the man of the match. 'We have the chance of going to Twickenham next and winning the triple crown. We have to be confident.' Gatland took heart from Wales's ability to overcome the loss of North and Bennett without any adverse effect. 'It shows how we have matured as a side,' he said. 'We were without Sam and Bradley as well and the players are able to take disruption in their stride and not let it get to them psychologically. Everyone seemed to write off Scotland, but we knew they would be dangerous. They came to play rugby and they put us under a lot of pressure. We ran and carried the ball well in the first half but could not hold on to it. The message at half-time was to keep things simple, retain possession and the chances would come. That is what happened. We were much more accurate in the second half and we upped the tempo. We scored three tries and would have had a couple more if the centres had passed the ball. We are pleased with the result given that we were without three or four key players.'

Wales were one victory away from the triple crown and

comparisons were being made with the 2008 side under Gatland who in their second match had enjoyed a similar victory over Scotland, 30–15. 'I think this team is a bit more advanced than four years ago,' said Shaun Edwards. 'We played England at Twickenham first up then in our first game together and there was not a huge amount of understanding among the players about what we wanted. If we can keep our discipline and avoid costly sin-bins, we can be excited about going there. Scotland provided excellent preparation for Twickenham because they were combative at the breakdown, as England will be, looking to upset our rhythm. They will try to get to Mike Phillips, and that is what Scotland did at times.'

Wales moved to the top of the table, ahead of England on points difference, with both sides having a 100 per cent record. France were also undefeated, but they had only played one match. Twickenham loomed not just as the final leg of the quest for the triple crown but as a potential title decider, although England had to go to Paris in the following round. That Lydiate was named man of the match showed how Wales's game was evolving: for all their power and finishing ability behind – their six tries had all been scored by three-quarters – their defence was as crucial. A trait of New Zealand over the years was that they had been at their most dangerous when the opposition was in possession, forcing turnovers and attacking disorganised defences. 'The tough one for us will be at Twickenham against an England side that has not shown much at the moment,' said Shane Williams, who had traded his boots for a seat in the BBC studio. 'The triple crown is on and the confidence is there. We can go to Twickenham and win against an English side that is not playing the best rugby at the moment. The good thing for Wales is that there is more to come from them.' Wales had only won at Twickenham once since 1988, but it was a ground that held sweet memories for Gatland and Edwards from their trophy-drenched days with Wasps. Wales would be the favourites and it was not a prospect that spooked the coaches.

4

Home Is Where the Art Is

Every ceiling, when reached, becomes a floor, upon which one walks as a matter of course and prescriptive right.

Aldous Huxley

SHANE WILLIAMS HAD SAID BEFORE THE TOURNAMENT that the England match was the one he feared the most. His apprehension about Wales's prospects at Twickenham was understandable. Wales would be going there as favourites for the first time since 1988, with England not so much in a state of transition, after a World Cup campaign that took up as much space on the news pages as it did in sports sections, as virtually starting from new. The average score in the fixture between 1990 and 2010, including a friendly in 2007, was England 37 Wales 13, with the home side winning on each occasion except 2008, the opening game in Wales's grand slam campaign that year. That was Gatland's first match in charge: England had made the World Cup final the previous year and Wales had been knocked out at the pool stage, prompting the Welsh Rugby Union to sack the head coach Gareth Jenkins and scour the southern hemisphere before hiring Gatland. England had been the firm favourites that day, a billing they lived up to in the opening half when they led 16–6. They would have been almost out of sight but for a try-saving tackle on the wing Paul Sackey by the hooker Huw Bennett just before the interval. Bennett was one of thirteen Ospreys in Wales's starting line-up that day, a number that had shrivelled to three by the time of the 2012 fixture, while Mike Phillips, Adam Jones and Alun Wyn Jones, who was recalled after making two appearances for Ospreys following an operation on his big toe, were the only survivors from the team that took the field at the start of the 2008 Six Nations. Bennett's 2012 campaign had ended against Scotland: he went off after ten minutes for repairs to a cut ear, but after returning he suffered an Achilles tendon injury and Ken Owens replaced him at Twickenham, the fifth hooker to be chosen by Gatland in less than a year after Matthew Rees, Bennett, Lloyd Burns and Richard Hibbard, who all suffered various spells out of action through injury.

Bennett, who announced before the end of the 2012 campaign that he was joining the players who were based in France after agreeing a contract with Lyon, was one of seven players in the Wales squad who had had the option of making themselves available for England. He was born in Ebbw Vale and educated at Clevedon in North Somerset. He played for England Schools, alongside future Red Rose internationals Olly Barkley, Nick Duncombe and James Simpson-Daniel, but there was only one country he wanted to represent at senior level. In a match programme interview, he commented, 'I could not play for Wales at school level because of where I was being educated, but there was never any danger of me pursuing a senior career with England. I never considered it, because I was Welsh.'

Three of Wales's three-quarter line in the 2012 Six Nations were born in England: Alex Cuthbert in Gloucester, George North in King's Lynn and Jonathan Davies in

Solihull. The fourth, Jamie Roberts, arrived not too far from the English border in Newport: the city's rugby club has dual membership of the Welsh Rugby Union and the Rugby Football Union. North's family moved to Anglesey in north Wales, where his mother, Jan, was born, when he was two. He started playing rugby because of his brother. 'He went off to play for Llangefni when he was quite young and came back ranting and raving about it,' said North in a television interview during the 2012 tournament. 'I was the jealous brother and wanted in, so I went down and I never looked back. I started in the back row, playing at six or seven, but as I grew bigger and faster and had a few little injuries, I decided I did not want my face smashed in week in, week out and ended up on the wing.' He played for Pwllheli and Rhyl at youth level before being spotted by the Scarlets and brought into their academy. He went to Llandovery College, capped by Wales at Under-18 level, and became a semi-professional player with Llandovery RFC. He made his debut for the Scarlets in the then Magners League in September 2010, five months after his 18th birthday. He was on the losing side against Treviso, but he scored two tries, using his speed for the first and his strength for the second, carrying defenders over the line. Gatland took note, saying on television: 'I have heard a lot about him already and he was very impressive. If he keeps playing like that every week, he is definitely going to catch the eye. It is about taking his opportunities and being consistent.'

North was not watching Gatland being interviewed. 'I had a phone call from my mother, who told me to turn the television on because Warren Gatland was talking about me,' said North in September 2010. 'It is nice to get recognition from the head coach of your country, but I am not putting too much into it. If I am able to play for Wales, it would be an absolute dream come true for me, but all I am looking for at the moment is to nail down a place in the Magners League with the Scarlets, something I am still pinching myself about, and to represent Wales at my age group in the Under-20s. Anything after that would just be an absolutely massive bonus.' North's impressive start for the Scarlets had alerted England because of his dual qualification but, asked if he would welcome any approach from across the border, he said simply: 'No.' Within three months, he was playing for Wales against South Africa and, as on his league debut, scoring two tries. He was Wales's most talked about player during the 2011 World Cup, commentators billing him as the new Jonah Lomu and former All Blacks saying that Wales had to be considered potential winners of the tournament because of the variety of their threat behind the scrum: the power of North and Roberts, the wizardry of Shane Williams and Leigh Halfpenny, the opportunism of Jonathan Davies and a pair of half-backs in Mike Phillips and Rhys Priestland who were tactically sharp.

'Looking back on the World Cup, it was an incredible experience,' said North in a revealing interview in *The Independent* at the end of 2011, 'but I'm treating it as a stepping stone. I want to play in the next one, in 2015, and to do that I have to meet the standards I've set myself, which are very high. I know Scarlets will help in that – the people at the club do a fantastic job in keeping me grounded – but I'll drive myself, too. There's an OCD side to me when it comes to rugby: if I don't play well, I go through the whole game in my head before I go home, work out where I went wrong, then sit down and go through it on tape. I never feel I'm done. There's always something I can do better, something more to achieve.' He admitted that it had taken him a while to get over the semi-final defeat to France. 'If I'm honest, I didn't think the French had much substance that day. There are times when you think: if they're really on their game, our chances of winning are pretty slim. It wasn't like that in Auckland. Even after we lost Sam Warburton [sent off for a dangerous tackle], there was never a point when I thought they had much to throw at us, that they could hurt us. To lose in the way we did was pure frustration. At the end, I was so tired I could barely walk. I was certainly too knackered to talk to anyone. I just lay down on the floor of the changing-room and stayed there for half an hour, silent. It was the worst I'd ever felt about rugby. My mum and dad had been in New Zealand for the pool stage and had reserved tickets to go back if we made the final. That defeat saved them a fortune. Believe me, there was nothing else good about it.'

Like North, Jonathan Davies never had any intention of exploiting his England qualification. His parents moved back to Wales when he was six months old and he grew up in the Fox and Hounds pub in Bancyfelin, a village with a population of 300 on the main road between Carmarthen and St Clears. It has a sporting pedigree out of all proportion to its size, producing five Welsh rugby internationals, including Mike Phillips and Delme Thomas, a member of Wales's grand-slam-winning team in 1971, the Olympic gold-medal-winning cyclist Geraint Thomas and Vince Thomas, Delme's uncle, who was a boxing champion in the 1930s. 'My nationality has never been an issue for me,' said Davies in an interview with *Rugby World* in the summer of 2011. 'I see myself as Welsh.' He started playing rugby when he was at primary school, moving to centre after his coach considered him too big to be an outside-half. He made his debut for the Scarlets when he was eighteen and made his Wales debut as a twenty-one year old on the 2009 tour to Canada and the United States, scoring two tries against the latter. He started the Tests against

Argentina and Australia at the end of that year, partnering Roberts in the midfield, but only made two appearances in 2010, on tour against the All Blacks, as Gatland used James Hook in the midfield. He played in four of the five matches in the 2011 Six Nations, though, when Hook was used mostly at outside-half, and started in every one of Wales's seven matches in the World Cup, partnering Roberts each time and scoring three tries, including the one that clinched victory over Ireland in the quarter-final.

'Being involved in the 2011 Six Nations helped my confidence and made me feel part of the squad more,' he said, before comparing himself to Scott Gibbs, the former Wales and Lions centre who had denied England the grand slam in 1999 with a late try at Wembley; it was to be another Scott who thwarted England at Twickenham in 2012. 'Scott Gibbs was perhaps similar to the way I play,' said Davies. 'Some of the stuff he did was so dynamic and really exciting to watch; it's something I'd like to do myself. He was a lot more skilful than some people thought and I hope I can show that myself, too. The competition for places is fierce with Wales and we are working at such a high level now in training. The squad is pretty grounded. We all know there is a lot of expectation on us, but I think we can handle that. There is a good feeling within the group and we know what is expected on the field. We are all working hard and doing our jobs, and we are not going away from that.' Davies was to give Gatland a boost after the England match by signing a new two-year contract with the Scarlets. He had been coveted by clubs in France and England, and while most of the players who had left Wales or who were about to were closer to the end of their careers than the beginning, at 23 Davies's career was still on the rise.

'There was a period where it was a tough decision,' he

said after the announcement of his new contract. 'It was chopping and changing quite a lot for a few weeks and it was a difficult time because it was always on your mind. You wanted to get it sorted because people were asking you about it all the time. I just kept my head down and made sure that I made the right decision. I spoke to my family and had a meeting with the coaches in Llanelli and some other people as well. It put me in a tight spot, but I saw that I was at a stage in my career where I was still developing. The other boys who are leaving are probably more experienced. It was key for my development to stay in Wales and the best place to do that is the Scarlets because of the exciting back division we have there and the relationship I have with the coaches.'

The other three players in the Wales squad who were, at the start of their careers, qualified to play for England were all back rowers: Dan Lydiate, Aaron Shingler and Sam Warburton. Lydiate was born in Salford, the son of a farmer from Manchester and a mother from mid Wales; Shingler was born in Aldershot and was also eligible to play for Scotland before representing Wales in Sevens. Warburton was a Cardiffian, but his father was born in London and his paternal grandparents lived in Yorkshire. He was plucked from relative obscurity by Gatland and named in the squad for the 2009 tour to Canada and the United States. He had played a few matches for Cardiff Blues earlier in the year after recovering from shoulder reconstruction surgery. He had played for Wales at every level from the Under-16s upwards before turning out for Glamorgan Wanderers in the Welsh Premiership. If his original selection by Gatland was unexpected, it was nothing compared to the surprise the coach generated when he named Warburton as captain for the game against the Barbarians in June 2011 in place of the injured Matthew Rees; the player himself was among those shocked. 'I noticed I had a missed call on my phone and it was Warren,' recalled Warburton. 'I wondered why he was ringing me and when I spoke to him he said: "Do you want to be captain for the Barbarians game?" I remember laughing because I was so shocked. I put the phone down and stood still for ten seconds, taking it all in. I told my Dad, who is a bit of a nerdy statistician. He said there had only ever been something like 122 captains of Wales ever. I was one of them and felt very privileged.'

Captaincy was not new to Warburton, who had led Wales at Under-19 and Under-20 levels. He skippered the Under-20s in the 2008 Junior World Championship, which was held in Wales, having inspired the Under-19s to the semi-final of their World Championship twelve months before, and they reached the last four, losing to New Zealand 31–6 in the semi-final. The team included Halfpenny, Jonathan Davies, Justin Tipuric and Rhys Webb, who all featured in the 2012 Six Nations.

The 2008 Junior World Championship was a competition that Warren Gatland had watched with interest. Writing in the tournament programme, he said that he had already informed the Under-20s that some of them could well find themselves at the Rugby World Cup in 2011. Pointing out that these young players' performances would be a test of Welsh rugby development's progress, he stated that one of his aims as coach was to ensure that success at junior level would bear fruit on the senior international stage.

Warburton and Jonathan Davies were to go on the Wales senior squad's tour in 2009, when a number of players were in South Africa with the Lions, but Halfpenny won his senior cap in the autumn of 2008. He had taken Wales into the semi-finals with a late try and conversion against France in the final match of the group stage, although his next knockout meeting with Les Bleus was not to end as sweetly. Dan Biggar, the Ospreys outside-half, was also to feature in Wales's autumn programme in 2008. Patrick Horgan, the Under-20 coach in 2008, singled out Warburton at the end of the championship. 'Sam is just physically on a different level to anything I've ever seen,' he said. 'He could play regional rugby, without a shadow of a doubt, right now. Next summer I would expect him to be on the Wales tour, irrespective of how much regional rugby he has played.'

As he pondered Gatland's telephone call about the captaincy, Warburton struggled to understand why he had been chosen. In an interview that was printed in the match programme at Twickenham in 2012, he confided that he hadn't previously considered himself captain material, although he thought that perhaps his rigorous attitude to training had played a part in his selection for the role. He stated that he'd resolved his doubts by deciding simply to be himself, saying, 'The game against the Barbarians was a big learning curve and I realised after it that the most important thing is not to try and change what you already do.' As captain, he said, it was important to find the right balance between being selfish enough to ensure he got his own preparations right and looking out for everyone else. He also had words of praise for his teammates, describing a close-knit group of young men with a shared outlook on rugby and life.

Fixtures between Wales and England had, over the years, been marked by ill-feeling: 1980 and 1987 were prime examples. It was the one fixture, above any other in the Six Nations, that Welsh supporters wanted their team to win. After Wales had been beaten by the All Blacks in the 1987 World Cup semi-final, their then manager Clive Rowlands remarked that they could always go back to beating England every year. Warburton, hardly surprisingly given his background, was an atypical

Welshman in that he never indulged in any anti-English sentiment. 'Although I never thought about making myself available for England, I did support them in the 2003 World Cup,' said Warburton in an interview with *The Guardian* before the first of two World Cup warm-up matches against England in 2011. 'My grandmother has a broad Yorkshire accent: I am not like a lot of Welshmen who have an anti-English attitude, even if I am just as eager for us to beat them on Saturday.'

Warburton was educated at Whitchurch High School in Cardiff, a contemporary of Gareth Bale, the Wales and Tottenham Hotspur footballer. 'I was a massive Spurs fan then and still am,' said Warburton. 'The irony was that Gareth supported Arsenal then. I was in school with him from year seven to year eleven. We were in the same group of mates and I was in quite a few classes with him, so I used to come across him a fair bit. We played in the school football team. My claim to fame is he once said that if I wasn't playing in defence we wouldn't win! I used to play centre-back or central midfield sometimes. I was a good school player, but I don't think I would ever have made a living out of football and I was certainly not in Gareth's class: he was the best footballer I have ever seen. I did have Cardiff City trials when I was 14, but it made me realise how far off I was: the boys there were much better than I was. That sort of made me realise rugby was my best chance.' Warburton expanded on his love of Tottenham Hotspur in the 2012 programme. 'If you asked me which stadium I would love to play in other than the Millennium Stadium it would be White Hart Lane and which team I would want to beat it would be Arsenal,' he said. He described his Spurs-themed childhood bedroom and declared that if he got another dog he planned to call it Harry after Tottenham manager Harry Redknapp. Coincidentally, Spurs were playing Arsenal in the north

London derby at the Emirates Stadium the day after Wales's date at Twickenham. As the game kicked off, Warburton was being interviewed in Wales's hotel in the Vale of Glamorgan. He missed his side scoring the opening two goals, but was back in front of the television to see Arsenal netting five without reply.

Warburton devoted himself to rugby from the age of 15, though not to the point where it made his education suffer: he declined an approach to play for Wales in a world-series Sevens event because he did not want to disrupt his A-level studies. 'You have to make a decision when you are 15 or 16,' he told the *South Wales Echo* before Wales's tour to North America in 2009. 'I still like to play a bit of football, but rugby has definitely taken over now and I absolutely love playing the game. My favourite position is seven and that's where I'd like to be in the long term. I started out there at school, then I was chucked into the second row for a bit, which I hated, although I guess it was good for the physical side of my game. Then I went back to the back row as soon as Wales Schools kicked in and I've played there at every age-grade covering six to eight. I'm comfortable anywhere in the back row, but to play at number 8 nowadays, you've got to be 6 ft 4 in. I'm not going to end up at 17 or 18 stone; that's not my body size. So I think seven is going to be where I finish up.'

Warburton became Wales's first choice at seven at the start of 2011, playing in all five matches of that year's Six Nations. Martyn Williams was left out of the squad and, at the age of 35, his international career had stalled on 98 caps. He was to make one more appearance, leading the team against Argentina in the last of the World Cup warm-ups, and he was on the opposite side to Warburton when Wales played the Barbarians, chosen by the invitation club to give Gatland the opportunity of judging the two open-sides together, something he had not been able to do away from the training field because they both played for the Blues. Williams was still the first choice ahead of Warburton at regional level, but as he looked ahead to the World Cup Gatland felt that the nature of the position the pair were competing for had changed. Williams had relied more on his speed across the field and presence of mind in his career than physique, but the advent of counter-rucking had placed an increasing premium on size and power. Gatland was unusually terse when asked in May 2011 why he had given Warburton the captaincy, saying merely that he was one of the leaders in the squad who would benefit from the experience of leading the side, but there appeared to be two factors. Warburton was assured of his place in the starting line-up and Gatland had, slowly but surely, opted for youth ahead of experience, promoting players who had not been scarred by failure. The coach was frustrated by a perception outside the squad that they would be playing for second place behind South Africa in their World Cup pool and that their priority should be defeating Samoa and Fiji. Williams, like the outside-half Stephen Jones, who won his 100th cap against the Barbarians, had been a fixture for Wales for more than a decade and had been on three Lions tours. He had been part of the 2005 and 2008 grand slams and was a player Warburton looked up to. But experience was no longer seen as a virtue. Gatland turned to players he could mould, such as the Newport Gwent Dragons number 8 Toby Faletau, a 20 year old who made his debut against the Barbarians and who was chosen for the World Cup squad.

Williams was typically gracious after being supplanted by Warburton. 'I am not surprised at all by how well Sam has done,' he said before playing for the Barbarians. 'He's a very level-headed player, an intelligent player as well, and it is by no means going to be his only game as captain. I have no doubt that he'll do it a fair few times in the future. With some players you might be a little bit concerned that it will go to their heads or they will go into the comfort zone. But that's nothing like Sam at all. He works as hard as anybody, not only at the physical side of it but on the technical and analysis sides as well. I think going to the World Cup is now a long shot for me. There is no room for sentiment in the professional game: you should not be there unless you warrant your place. If I do not play for Wales again, I will be happy with what I have achieved.'

Gatland made the right call at the right time, even if Williams cruelly missed out on the distinction of joining the small number of players who had won 100 caps for his country, stranded on 99. Warburton not only led Wales in the World Cup after Matthew Rees was ruled out by injury but did so with such presence and dignity – impressing even the International Rugby Board by the way he conducted himself at the disciplinary hearing after he had been sent off in the semi-final against France – there was no doubt he would be the captain for years to come, barring injury. Sir Ian McGeechan, one of the most experienced coaches in Britain through his time with the Lions, Scotland and various clubs, was among those who made Warburton his man of the tournament. Warburton had become the youngest captain of a team in the quarter-finals of a World Cup when Wales played Ireland and in their opening game of the tournament, against South Africa, he outplayed Heinrich Brussow, one of the best fetchers in the game, and won six turnovers, justifying Gatland's assertion before the match that by the time the World Cup was over, Warburton would have achieved stardom. 'Somebody who does not know the first thing about rugby would understand that Sam is doing exceptionally well,' said Shaun Edwards before the quarter-final. 'His leadership for a 22 year old is very mature. He's everything you want in a modern-day professional athlete: he's teetotal, he looks after his body and he's had a really good, strong, injury-free run, which in the past he hasn't really had. He dominated the breakdowns against South Africa even though he was up against one of the best open-sides in the world.' The former Wales and Lions captain Mervyn Davies, whose death in March 2012 overshadowed Wales's grand slam match against France, felt Warburton had presided over a culture change. 'Long may it continue,' he went on. 'I do not see how the captaincy can be taken off him now. He has played out of his skin and he has incredible maturity for such a young man. Wales could not ask for any more from a captain.'

England had a player who the previous year had been asked to make himself available for Wales. Ben Morgan was a Bristol-born number 8 who was in his second season with the Scarlets having joined from Merthyr via the Blues. In the summer of 2011 he was contacted by Gatland and asked if he would be interested in making himself available for Wales when he qualified on the grounds of residency at the beginning of 2012. He also received a call from Martin Johnson, who was then the England team manager, asking if he would play for the Saxons, England's second team, that summer. He declined Johnson's invitation but deferred making a decision on his international future until the end of the year. 'I was in shock,' he said. 'I talked it over with my family and friends, but I had so many people telling me what to do or what might be best for me that I had no head space to think for myself. By putting the decision off, it meant that everyone went away and it allowed me to reflect. When I had that time, it was an easy decision because I am English: I was born in England, I have always supported England. A country is different to a club. If you are going to take it to the next level, it has to be for the right reasons, particularly as you have to push yourself that much harder. It has to be coming from the heart to start with. When England won the World Cup in 2003, I was sitting in my local club in Dursley cheering them on. I could not imagine myself lining up for Wales against England at Twickenham and not singing "God Save the Queen". It would not have been right.'

Morgan announced a month before the start of the 2012 Six Nations that he would be available for England, a team that was then under the interim charge of Stuart Lancaster, the Saxons' coach the previous summer. He was immediately named in the 32-strong England elite squad and made his international debut against Scotland at Murrayfield, coming off the bench in the second half and making an impact, as he did against Italy in Rome the following week. Gatland had liked the impact made by Morgan with the ball in hand, but that role in the Wales team had been filled by Faletau. There was a greater opportunity for Morgan with England, who were shedding a layer of skin after the World Cup, but his decision was not based on who was the more likely to cap him first. 'Nobody can question Ben for setting his sights on the pride and dream of playing for his home country,' said the Scarlets' head coach, Nigel Davies. 'He has always had raw ability and pace, stocky, big-boned, extremely explosive and very difficult to handle. When he came to us he was carrying a bit too much weight. We have moved him on from just being a ball-carrier to being far more effective in other aspects of his game and he has shown great determination to take his rugby career forward.'

Morgan, the first Scarlet to play for England, was chosen to start against Wales and acknowledged his debt to Davies and the Scarlets. 'I had never been in an academy system and when it came to diet, I ate what I liked and liked what I ate,' he said. 'It took a lot of hard work to get me into shape [he was around 21 stone when he arrived in Llanelli] and some of the work was gruelling but it has paid off. I am now at my optimum weight for strength, speed and endurance and, again, I have so much to thank the Scarlets for. The style of play here is based on open and expansive rugby, which suits me. I just love getting my hands on the ball, but you also have to be able to adapt when play becomes tight.' His decision to opt for England alerted Premiership clubs and before the end of the Six Nations, Gloucester had agreed a transfer fee with the Scarlets.

Morgan was among a number of new faces in an England squad that had been overhauled after the World Cup. Wales had been used to campaigns that ended in miserable failure, having three times missed out on the knockout stage, but England's failure was not so much on the field, although their exit in the quarter-finals marked their least successful tournament since 1999, as off it. They topped their group with a 100 per cent record and they returned home with an 80 per cent success record, compared to Wales's 57 per cent, but their time in New Zealand was largely spent firefighting with stories about their players regularly appearing on the news pages. They appeared a squad divided and their rugby was uninspiring. Johnson had never attempted to court the media since his appointment in the summer of 2008 and payback time had come. His media conferences during the World Cup became concerned less and less with rugby and the playing of the game and far more with what some of his players had been up to in their spare time. England had arrived in Auckland as the Six Nations champions, missing out on the grand slam after being well beaten by Ireland in Dublin in their final match, but there were signs in their two warm-up matches against Wales that there were fault-lines in their game. Although the matches were both won by the home side, Wales looked markedly fitter, a legacy of their training camps in Poland, but also tactically smarter. England had most of the play in the match at the Millennium Stadium, but they hammered and banged away at the Wales line with no subtlety and less finesse, and they failed to score a try. They had managed two at Twickenham seven days before in a 23–19 victory, but conceded three. 'I thought our fitness levels showed in the last 20 minutes,' said Warburton after the first encounter. 'England were pretty flat and they were hanging on. We struggled to score tries in the Six Nations and to get three against a side that defended well was an achievement.'

The Welsh Rugby Union had gone through torrid periods in the 1980s and 1990s, culminating in the overthrow of its general committee in 1993, but the civil war at the Rugby Football Union in 2011, which started with the sacking of the chief executive John Steele after a dispute, played out in the media, about the appointment of a performance director: some on the governing body wanted to see the return of Sir Clive Woodward, the coach when England won the World Cup in 2003, to take charge of the department and become the line manager of whoever was in charge of the senior national side. Gatland, who had twice been sounded out by the RFU in 2007 through intermediaries about whether he would be interested in coaching England, said when the RFU first advertised the position of performance director at the beginning of 2011 that he would not want to report to such a figure but have a direct link to his chief executive, as he had in Wales. Personality got in the way of process at Twickenham and before the year was out it did not have a permanent chief executive or a chairman of its board of directors. It needed someone to take charge of England.

Johnson, whose contract was up at the end of the year, resigned five weeks after England returned home as the

RFU conducted an inquiry into what had happened in New Zealand. Mike Tindall, England's captain in the opening group match against Argentina, had been fined £25,000 and thrown out of the elite squad after a night out in Queenstown, James Haskell and Chris Ashton were reprimanded for bad behaviour and Manu Tuilagi, the centre who had made a try-scoring debut against Wales at Twickenham before the World Cup, was fined for jumping off a ferry in Auckland harbour. In addition, two of the management team had been banned from the final group game for switching the ball before Jonny Wilkinson attempted a conversion. 'I think it is in the interests of both the England team and myself not to carry on,' said Johnson. 'I have a choice at the moment. If I hadn't made that decision, someone may have made it for me. I haven't been let down [by his players]. We toured together. Things get reported, but I don't think it was an accurate representation. It made it difficult for us, but how much it affected things on the field, no one could answer that.'

Johnson had been a controversial appointment because he had had no managerial, or coaching, experience when he was approached to replace Brian Ashton, who had guided England to the World Cup final in 2007. The RFU had not got around to thinking about his successor when the various reports the inquiry team were considering were leaked to *The Times*, which, for three successive days, laid bare the rifts within the squad. Johnson was generally supported, but his coaching team, with the exception of Graham Rowntree, was ridiculed. One of the complaints, which contrasted with how Gatland had managed Wales, was that the worst example was set by some of the senior players. 'They treated it like an old-school tour and did not take it seriously,' complained one player. 'If it's the senior players leading drinking games or drinking until they can't remember anything, what example are the younger players set?' asked another. Words like mindless, reckless, unacceptable, disrespectful and immature were employed. And a comparison was made with Wales. 'I watched the coaches umming and ahhing for ages about whether to let Nick Mullins and Phil Vickery [the ITV commentators] watch training. The next day, the same commentators go to Wales and get made a cup of tea and welcomed in. Is it any wonder they feel like we treat them like s*** and do the same back to us?'

The upshot was that the RFU lacked the time to find a permanent head coach before the start of the Six Nations and Lancaster was asked to fill the position for the duration of the tournament. The World Cup captain Lewis Moody announced his retirement from international rugby, along with Jonny Wilkinson, and while Tindall was reinstated to the elite squad on appeal, he had little chance of being named in the revised 32 in the new year. With Steve Thompson forced to end his career because of injury, Andrew Sheridan unavailable, Haskell in Japan and Simon Shaw off to France, England were shorn of experience. Rowntree and Andy Farrell, the Saracens' backs coach, were appointed to assist Lancaster, who quickly aborted the planned pre-Six Nations training camp in Portugal and relocated the squad to Leeds, saying it was important for the squad to regain public trust and to do that they needed to go to the grassroots. He used the word humility on several occasions, acknowledging that the national set-up had come to be perceived as arrogant, and he had an inclusive policy towards the media, making reporters feel involved again.

While the RFU said that Lancaster would be a contender for the permanent position of head coach if he applied, the advertisement the governing body put out pointed to a coach of proven international experience and track record being appointed, as if it were apologising for turning to Johnson in 2008. Little was expected of England in the Six Nations with France, Wales and Ireland backed by the bookmakers to finish ahead of them. Their first two matches were away to the weakest teams in the tournament, Scotland and Italy, and they had to travel to France in the fourth round. England had never won three matches on the road in a Six Nations campaign, but they got off to a winning start at Murrayfield, showing the team spirit they had been lacking in the World Cup, and they eventually overcame Italy in a cold Olympic Stadium in Rome. They did not create much in either match, but they were defensively strong, with the newcomer Brad Barritt making an impact in the centre outside Owen Farrell, and they were clearly buying into Lancaster's new and more austere culture.

They were not, though, expected to be more than a speed bump on Wales's journey to the title. The former Wales outside-half turned television commentator Jonathan Davies, not to be confused with the Wales centre of the same name, caused a stir when he said: 'I do not think we have gone to Twickenham before and out-muscled England, but the side we have now we could go there and absolutely smash them physically. The English pack does not strike fear into anyone. They are a good club side who are growing together, but there isn't anyone outstanding in there. Tom Croft will have a go at our lineout but our back row is better, our second row is better, our front row is bigger and our centres are bigger. We could absolutely go to town on them. England are a young team and they have shown a lot of spirit. Defensively they are solid, but offensively they haven't created anything yet. I spoke to Stuart Lancaster before the tournament and he wanted to play an expansive game, with Ben Youngs dictating play, but that hasn't happened.'

Croft reacted indignantly to the comments, and two

salient facts that were overlooked in the rush to make Wales the overwhelming favourites were that their record winning margin at Twickenham was twelve points, back in 1976, and England had never lost a Six Nations match in front of their own supporters by more than seven points.

As Wales gathered at the beginning of the week, Rob Howley disputed that Wales should be regarded as the favourites. 'England are above us in the world rankings and possibly at home they should be favourites,' he said. 'The challenge is to rise to expectations: Jonathan Davies used the word physically after smashed when talking about the game, but we know how good England can be. They have played good sides in very difficult conditions. With a back three of Chris Ashton, Ben Foden and David Strettle they can stretch any defensive line with the ball in hand. We are mindful of how they can play and it is about us not allowing them to do that. You have to take games in the Six Nations in isolation: momentum is important, but this is a derby game, a one-off. England will be targeting us. You are only as good as your next game: we left 20 points out on the park against Scotland and we might not have the fortune to have so many opportunities at Twickenham. We have to earn the right to play.'

Warburton, who had recovered from the dead leg that forced him to miss the victory over Scotland, said the weekend would show whether Wales were comfortable dealing with expectation. 'If you aim to be successful, as Wales do, you cannot be content with being underdogs all the time,' he went on. 'England are always difficult to beat. I am not sure what happened to them in the World Cup: before the tournament I thought they had it in them to make the final, having won the Six Nations and beaten Australia the previous autumn. I was surprised by the way it went for them, but they only lost one game and qualified for the quarter-finals at the head of their group. In no way could they be described as a bad side. Playing England is not unlike facing South Africa: you wake up the following morning feeling you have been hit by a train. They are very physical, strong in the set-pieces and have a good go-forward. People have criticised their style, but the beauty of rugby for me is that there are many ways of playing. Scotland posed a different threat to the one we had encountered in Ireland a week before and England will be different again. It would be pretty dull if everyone played the same. We have started well, with six tries from our three-quarters in our two games, but we know we still have work to do. We have in no way fulfilled our potential.'

Both sides made changes after victories. Warburton was back to lead Wales, Owens replaced Bennett and Alun Wyn Jones returned to the second row for his first appearance since the World Cup. Tuilagi returned to the England midfield after recovering from a hamstring strain. Farrell moved from centre to outside-half, where he partnered Lee Dickson, who was brought in for the out-of-form Ben Youngs. At forward, Morgan was preferred to Phil Dowson, and Geoff Parling replaced Tom Palmer in the second row. The changes meant that England had players in the key positions of 8, 9 and 10 who were all making their first international appearances at Twickenham, and they were joined by Barritt, Parling, the captain Chris Robshaw and Mouritz Botha. The starting line-up had 188 caps between them, less than twice the number accumulated by Stephen Jones, who a day before the match had replaced the chicken-pox infected James Hook on the bench. 'The players are excited to be playing at home and want to put in a performance,' said Lancaster. Asked about the prospect of England being smashed physically, he replied: 'We will bring our physicality to the party I am sure. We have a number of players making their first appearances for England at home and it is exciting for them. You cannot dip your toe in the water; you have to dive straight in.'

Much was made in the build-up of Wales's giant back division, but Howley stressed that size without skill was not worth much. 'I think skill in international rugby is so important,' he said. 'Test rugby is about creating space and putting the ball into it. Rugby is a passing game and we have stressed to our players that while you need physicality, you have to be able to create space. You can have seven backs who are 6 ft 6 in. and 19 st., but if they cannot pass the ball into space, what use are they? It is a balance of having size, speed and skill. I would like to think skill and speed come a little bit higher than physicality. It is all about combinations having time to get to know one another's strengths and weaknesses. Jonathan Davies and Jamie Roberts showed in the World Cup that they are a potent force: they can kick, pass and run, they have an innate ability to play off each other, and with Rhys putting them into areas, we have a combination of strengths. Jonathan's support lines are very good and he knows where to attack. He is very quick over the first six metres, deceptively so, and he sniffs out tries. Leigh Halfpenny is a special ingredient in the back three with his coolness and calmness under pressure and his work-rate off the ball. He is exceptional and if they all worked as hard as him we would have an even more potent back line.'

Gatland had antagonised England before the 2011 Six Nations match in Cardiff by questioning the temperament of the hooker Dylan Hartley, but he drenched them with compliments during his team announcement. 'Their management will be pleased with the character shown in their opening games. Discipline will be a key factor for us on the weekend and it is an area where England are strong. It is a big game for us and I hope it is the transformation of this team. We need to deliver a good performance. We have a group of players who are fit, skilful, honest, keen and they have a bit of size about them. They just want to express themselves, and there is a prize to be won.'

Wales were looking for their 20th triple crown, but never once had they achieved the feat on English soil. It was the start of a big weekend for Welsh sport. Many of the supporters travelling by road and rail from Wales were staying the night and going to Wembley the following day, where Cardiff City were meeting Liverpool in the final of the Carling Cup. In between, the Welsh boxer Nathan Cleverly was defending his WBO light-heavyweight title against the American Tommy Karpency in Cardiff.

England ran out to a cacophonous roar and they made the first play of the game when Morgan evaded Warburton and Farrell kicked towards Wales's 22. Priestland tried to run the ball back but Barritt, in a sign of what was to come, was quickly on him only for Farrell to be penalised for not rolling away. Priestland kicked for touch on the England 10-metre line, Warburton took the catch and immediately gave the ball to Phillips, who took advantage of a gap created by Morgan to bring in North on an angled run. The wing sprinted into the England 22 and had Ben Foden in front of him, but David Strettle, stretching out his left hand, clipped North's ankles. Priestland then chipped to the corner for Cuthbert, but the kick had too much weight on it. North was involved from the drop out, tackled into touch by the prop Alex Corbisiero. Wales were dominating possession, willing to run from their own half, and when England did have the chance of relief, they made mistakes, such as missing a penalty kick to touch and throwing crooked into an attacking lineout. Warburton was winning the breakdown and Wales attacked the gainline, making little impression on Barritt.

Wales were struggling to get the ball wide – Cuthbert received just two passes all afternoon – and almost incessant pressure had not yielded a point after eighteen minutes. When they eventually had a chance, Halfpenny was wide with a 30-metre penalty gained after England had buckled under pressure in a scrum.

When the first quarter ended, Wales had had 72 per cent of the possession, but England gained confidence from not conceding and they started taking the game to Wales through Tuilagi. They had been criticised for not showing any adventure in their first two matches, but Farrell switched play adroitly and their first sustained attack ended with Farrell kicking a penalty after Gethin Jenkins flopped off-side at a ruck. Halfpenny equalised within two minutes after England struggled to get the ball away from a breakdown and Botha was penalised for sealing off. When North tried to run after receiving the kick-off, he was immediately hauled down into touch by Parling and there were echoes in England's gameplan of the way Wales had played against Ireland in the World Cup quarter-final, tackling ball-carriers low before they had time to get into their stride and bringing them down. Wales found themselves sucked into a game they did not want and when England attacked from the lineout North had conceded, Strettle caused problems coming into the midfield and Barritt took out three defenders before the ball was moved to Tuilagi on the left. The centre was five metres from the line and the gap between the last two defenders Phillips and Cuthbert was too wide for either of them to make a tackle on him. Warburton, though, had read the danger and tackled Tuilagi sideways on, bringing him straight to the ground, and England had to settle for another penalty after Roberts, who was struggling with a knee injury he had picked up in the opening minutes, strayed off-side, earning himself a warning from the referee Steve Walsh.

England had mounted two attacks and gained points from each of them. Wales became more cautious, kicking possession away, and it needed a shirt-tugging tackle by Adam Jones on Croft to thwart a try-scoring opportunity. Wales were still causing problems at the breakdown and when Morgan prevented North from forcing a turnover, Halfpenny kicked the penalty from 45 metres to tie the scores. It was a full-blooded encounter and any notion that Wales would stroll to a record victory had been shattered. When Priestland, who had earlier been knocked backwards trying to tackle Tuilagi, was turned over trying to run the ball from his 22 after being denied time to kick, Warburton intercepted Chris Ashton's pass near his own line but Faletau went off his feet at the breakdown and Farrell kicked the penalty to give England a 9–6 lead at the break. Far from smashing England physically, Wales had been knocked back by Tuilagi, but a difference between the sides was that at times Wales showed artistry while England too often opted to kick in and around Wales's 22.

At half-time, Roberts was replaced by Scott Williams, another player who had been fast-tracked by Gatland. The Scarlet had made his debut as a replacement against the Barbarians in 2011 before he had become a regular with his region and made such an impact in the World Cup warm-ups that when Gavin Henson was ruled out of the tournament with a wrist injury the question was whether he would have been chosen ahead of Williams had he been fit. Priestland was carrying a knee problem that he had sustained during the warm-up. It was not the knee he had injured in January, and he only made the revelation after the end of the tournament, but he was visibly limping during the final match of the campaign against France. He was to endure his worst period as Wales's outside-half in the second period at Twickenham, targeted by England, who applied pressure on him and forced runners down narrow channels. It was pressure applied by Botha five minutes after the restart that had Wales staring at the prospect of defeat. England had been fortunate to gain a toehold in Wales's 22 because Dickson had got away with a knock-on as he retrieved the ball from a breakdown even though Walsh was a few metres away: the referee said the ball had gone backwards, which was the case, but only after it was dropped and bounced forward. Barritt's chip into Wales's 22 was covered by Halfpenny but, undecided between a desire to run the ball and a concern that he should kick it, he was caught in possession. Wales were slow to clear the ball from the breakdown, giving Botha the time to charge at Priestland. The outside-half kicked the ball straight, rather than to the right, and it hit Botha's outstretched arms. England looked set for their third chargedown try of the tournament, but the ball bounced sideways and when Botha picked it up he had no forward momentum and was tackled by Scott Williams three metres from the Wales line. England won the ruck, but as Corbisiero went to take advantage of an overlap on the left, created by Cuthbert coming off his wing to assist Williams, Priestland tackled the prop from an off-side position and forced a forward pass. Walsh, who had come close to sending Roberts to the sin-bin in the first half, had no hesitation in showing a yellow card to the outside-half who had prevented his side from conceding a potential seven points and it was the right decision. Farrell was presented with a penalty from in front of the posts, which he converted to make it 12–6, and Wales had to play for ten minutes with fourteen men. Six Nations statistics showed that Wales conceded more than seven points when they had a player in the sin-bin, more than any other side, and the last time they had been a man short at Twickenham, they shipped seventeen points. The match had reached its pivotal moment as Wales took the kick-off with 45 minutes and 30 seconds on the clock.

England kicked the ball to Halfpenny 16 seconds later. Williams and Jonathan Davies took play to England's 10-metre line and then Phillips took over, orchestrating a series of pick-and-gos, not a usual tactic of Wales's, but one that used up time. The next time England touched the ball there were 50 minutes exactly on the clock: Farrell kicked a penalty to touch from his own 10-metre line, awarded after Alun Wyn Jones had been blown for sealing off a ruck. Priestland had less than five minutes left in the sin-bin. England tried to drive the lineout but, after being shoved backwards, moved the ball to the right. Jonathan Davies flew out of the midfield and clattered into Farrell as the outside-half was about to pass. The ball went back to the halfway line, where Dickson fell on it. Davies arrived, stayed on his feet and scrambled for possession, forcing the scrum-half to hold on to the ball and concede a penalty. If England had had a break when Dickson knocked on, television replays showed that it was Wales's turn because the ball went forward off Davies's arm after he had tackled Farrell. 'I thought it came off his head,' Walsh could be heard saying.

Halfpenny failed to find touch with the penalty, but Ben Foden kicked the ball infield, Faletau went on a charge that left Farrell injured and when Hartley was caught off-side at a ruck, Halfpenny had a penalty from 35 metres just to the left of the posts and made it 12–9. When Farrell took the restart, after Wales had brought on Ryan Jones for Alun Wyn Jones, the game was 53 minutes and 59 seconds old. Priestland had 40 seconds left on the sidelines, time Wales used up keeping the ball in their 22. When he returned to the field Wales were no further behind than when he had left it and had won a psychological battle. Not that he made the immediate impact he intended: he was barged out of the way by Tuilagi and when he missed a penalty kick to touch it was punted back by Foden. Priestland received the ball just behind his own 10-metre line and shaped to pass only to spot Barritt hovering. He cut inside and was collared by Courtney Lawes, who had just replaced Botha, and Farrell. He failed to release the ball and was penalised, presenting Farrell with an opportunity 40 metres out in front of the posts. As the England outside-half addressed the ball, Gatland ordered Stephen Jones to start warming up. Priestland's time looked up on the ground where he had laid claim to the outside-half jersey less than seven months before.

Farrell pushed the kick wide and Priestland remained on the field. The sight of Jones, a 104-cap veteran who had originally been excluded from the Six Nations squad only to be called up when Priestland injured his knee, warming up may have been a motivational spur: Gatland was caught on camera speaking to Howley, who was wired up to the bench, immediately after Priestland conceded the penalty. 'We felt it was important that we showed faith in Rhys,' said Howley afterwards. 'Every player has a match when things do not go well for them, even Barry John suffered them, and the way Rhys responded in the last 15 minutes or so was telling. I had a long chat with him shortly after the game and the sign of a top player is how he responds to adversity. Rhys did so positively and we should not forget that he has only played international rugby at outside-half for a short time. He is learning all the time and you learn more about players from matches in which they have struggled than ones when they have been in top form.'

Priestland soon had to deal with a high kick from Foden. He was immediately caught by the England full-back but got the ball to Phillips, who cleared downfield. An outside-half did leave the field, but it was Farrell, who pulled up after dealing with a long diagonal from Priestland, who then chipped into space for North to collect and take play towards England's 22. When Wales were awarded a scrum Ben Youngs, who had replaced Dickson at scrum-half, tackled Faletau early. Walsh played advantage as Ryan Jones got over the gainline and Priestland's long pass gave Scott Williams the chance to run in between Tuilagi, who had been checked by North's decoy run in midfield, and Strettle. The centre had Foden in front of him with Halfpenny free on the outside, but he clattered into the full-back and was brought to ground. It was Wales's best opening of the second half and a rare instance in the tournament of poor decision-making under pressure. They had also used up their penalty advantage and when Gethin Jenkins was turned over by Matt Stevens five metres out, Wales found themselves back on the halfway line. Warburton won the lineout but appeared to be taken out in the air by his opposite number, Robshaw, who was penalised. Warburton, who had crashed to the ground awkwardly, got straight back to his feet, assisted by Hartley, and did not attempt to milk the incident, as Clerc had done when tip-tackled by the flanker in the World Cup semi-final. 'I had a bit of advice to stay down, but that would have been hypocritical given that I had been unimpressed at the way Clerc had reacted,' said Warburton, for whom honesty always would be the best policy. Replays showed that while Robshaw had made contact with him, Wales's lifters, Lydiate and Faletau, had got their timing wrong and were not there to bring their captain back down to ground. Walsh made the right call.

Priestland kicked the penalty into touch deep in England's 22. Warburton again won the lineout and Wales kept the ball for a series of drives. They were on England's 22 when Stevens tried to force another turnover but did so off his feet and was spotted by Walsh. There were nine minutes to go and Halfpenny levelled the scores. A bruising, physically gruelling and compelling match was reaching its conclusion. It was a time when Wales expected their fitness level to be telling: England emptied their bench while Gatland brought on only two players, Williams through injury and Ryan Jones on fifty-three minutes because Alun Wyn Jones had made only his second start in four months after surgery on a big toe. And it was England's replacements who had an influence on the outcome. Stevens conceded the equalising penalty and Youngs, with less than seven minutes left, wasted an opening on the right by passing to the feet of Lawes, who inadvertently kicked the ball forward. It was played in an off-side position by Rob Webber, a replacement for Hartley, and Wales, who had been scrambling in defence, were awarded a penalty on their own 10-metre line. Priestland found touch, Ryan Jones secured the ball but Priestland's high kick was marked by Foden. The full-back sliced his clearance in field; Halfpenny collected but was isolated in contact and was turned over by the ubiquitous Barritt and Tuilagi. Youngs looked to counter-attack just inside his own half with Wales stretched in defence. England had five players wide on the right but only Robshaw within range. The England captain fed the supporting Lawes, who was tackled by Warburton on the halfway line. He remained on his feet but Evans and Williams had arrived to wrestle for the ball and the replacement centre emerged with it. He ran with the ball for a couple of metres before noticing that the defence was flat because England had been on the attack. He kicked with the outside of his right foot into the 22 and found himself in a race with Croft for the bounce. The way he had grubbered the ball meant that it bounced away from Croft; had it gone towards the flanker, he would have got to it before Williams. As it was, it bounced perfectly for the centre, who stepped away from

Croft and dived over the line close to the posts; 75 minutes and 18 seconds had elapsed and Wales were ahead for the first time in the match. By the time Halfpenny added the conversion, England had less than four minutes to respond.

Wales had to secure the kick-off, but Croft took the ball as Cuthbert closed in. England needed to create a try, something they had not done all tournament, and they kept hold of the ball before Toby Flood, Farrell's replacement, chipped to the corner for Strettle to chase, but he was beaten to the bounce by North, who appeared to throw the ball into touch. England were awarded a lineout rather than a penalty; Croft took the catch but Adam Jones entered the driving maul from an off-side position and was penalised. England opted for another lineout: Parling's tap back went to ground and Youngs fell on the ball, five metres from Wales's line. England took play through four phases before Adam Jones tackled Stevens and was penalised for not rolling away. England again kicked to touch, on their left this time. There were 30 seconds left and they were playing for a draw. Parling caught the throw but Wales repulsed the initial driving maul only for England to roll again with Phil Dowson, a replacement for Morgan, getting to within three metres of the Wales line when Adam Jones collapsed the maul. 'I had to,' said Jones afterwards, 'otherwise England would have scored and the triple crown would have gone.' Walsh signalled that he was playing advantage, six seconds over the eighty minutes, but even though time was up, England would have one more play if the referee came back for the penalty. England drove on, Webber getting to within one metre of the line when Youngs moved the ball right to Flood. As three defenders moved in on the outside-half, he floated a long pass off his left hand to Mike Brown, Foden's replacement. North, outnumbered, had drifted off his wing, fearing the ball would go to Tuilagi. Brown had 12 metres to go but saw Jonathan Davies tracking across and passed, a fraction early, to Strettle outside him. The wing was five metres from the touchline with Halfpenny and Davies coming at him sideways, but rather than take the outside route, he cut back inside and was half-stopped by Halfpenny before Davies completed the tackle. Strettle landed just short of the line but stretched out his arm to touch the ball down and claimed the try. Walsh asked the touch judge Pascal Gauzere if he had had a good view and was told no. 'I think he was held up but I am going to have a check,' the referee said in reply before asking the television match official, Iain Ramage, to adjudicate. 'Iain, try or no try, please?' Walsh asked him, rather than was there any reason why he could not award a try. Ramage viewed the incident from several camera angles: the first appeared to show that North had thwarted the attempted touchdown; the second, from behind the posts, seemed to validate Strettle's argument; the third was inconclusive and the fourth revealed that while Strettle had got the ball over the line, he may have grounded it on his own arm. Video referrals were introduced to provide clarity, but each clip seemed only to confuse by offering contradictory evidence. The nature of Walsh's question meant that Ramage had to find incontrovertible proof that a try had been scored. He reported back after two minutes to say that he was still having a look. Thirty seconds later, he was ready: 'It is inconclusive that the ball was down,' he said. 'No try.' Walsh then asked: 'Iain, the next decision from that would clearly be scrum white feed five metres out, but what I am really getting at is was time up prior to that?' Ramage said, correctly: 'Time was up prior to the play.' Walsh responded: 'That's it? Call no side?' And he blew his whistle to end the contest. There were 83 minutes and 40 seconds on the match clock.

Home Is Where the Art Is

No mention was made of the fact Walsh had been playing advantage for Adam Jones's third offence in as many minutes. The time between Walsh raising his arm and Strettle getting to the Wales line was 21 seconds. Had he gone back for the penalty, Walsh would have been expected to have shown a yellow card to the Wales prop for persistently infringing and England would have had the option of a five-metre scrum against a pack a forward light. Had Brown's pass gone into touch rather than into Strettle's hands, England would have been given the penalty, but it was not the first time in the tournament that a referee playing advantage for a penalty had referred a possible try to the television match official. George Clancy had done so during Scotland's match against England when the home outside-half, Greig Laidlaw, kicked to the line immediately after Dan Cole had been caught off-side and claimed to have applied downward pressure. The try was not awarded, but Clancy did not go back for the penalty, giving England a drop-out. Scotland wondered afterwards whether he had forgotten he had been playing advantage and that question applied to Walsh. The International Rugby Board spoke to him the day after Wales's victory and he said he had deemed England to have gained a territorial advantage because they had got over the Wales line, although he was not picked up on his microphone saying advantage was over. It showed how arbitrary and loose the laws of the game could be: when Wales played Ireland in the 2011 Six Nations in Cardiff, the visitors thought they had scored a try after a long passage of play in which the referee Jonathan Kaplan had been playing advantage. It was ruled out for a forward pass, but Kaplan did go back for the penalty.

Strettle was adamant afterwards that he had touched the ball down, but England did not make too much of the incident. A try would have pulled them back to 19–17 and Flood would have had a conversion from the touchline to level the scores. 'It was unbelievable,' said Warburton after being named the man of the match. 'I don't think we played well at all. We knew it was going to be the toughest game of the Six Nations so far and we completely ignored everything that was being said in the media. We appreciated England were a quality outfit and, flipping heck, that was one hell of a Test match it was so tough. We have to be over the moon to come down here to get the triple crown: history shows you that this is a tough place. When we went down to 14 men, we wanted to keep the ball in the forwards and keep it tight. It was difficult because we did not have a second stand-off so Leigh had to fill in there and he did a great job. We did not want to throw it around and we did pretty well in the ten minutes Rhys was off the field. We believe we have got a really strong squad that can achieve things: we have Italy at home in two weeks, which is a must-win game, and we cannot afford to look any further ahead than that. We will enjoy this moment and then knuckle down again.'

Warburton went up to receive the triple crown trophy and the players posed for pictures, opening bottles of champagne and walking around the pitch, saluting the Welsh supporters, who were enjoying the moment. 'I don't know what to say,' said Scott Williams. 'I never thought I would come on and score the winning try. Our defence was superb. England threw everything at us but we stuck in there and managed to get the win.' And then it was off to the west car park, looking for a converted police van that held some cold discomfort. A team that had been questioned at the start of the month about what it had achieved at the World Cup and whether it had developed during the tournament had supplied some answers. Wales had turned a ceiling into a floor and had earned the right to walk on it. For the third match in a row, they had lost a key player to injury before the start of the second half – Warburton in Dublin, North against Scotland and Roberts at Twickenham – but they did not miss a step. 'That shows the maturity of the side,' said Howley, the day after the triple crown victory. 'We were not at our best against England but it was always going to be a game where the result was everything. The hype before it was that we were going to win at a canter. History told you it would not be and we knew just how difficult it would be to crack England. Winning at Twickenham is huge because it will give the players the confidence to take their game to the next level: we have come back from six points down in the second half away to Ireland and England, scoring a try in the last five minutes in both matches. England were good in defence and attack and really played as a team. It was a real Test match, one for the connoisseur.'

5

Parisse in the Springtime

There are moments when the many, through the few, become one.

Owen Sheers

WALES STAYED IN LONDON OVERNIGHT AFTER winning the triple crown, apart from Jamie Roberts who was driven home on the Saturday evening and ordered to rest his knee after suffering ligament damage for the third time since the World Cup. Two years before, they had travelled back from Twickenham a few hours after the end of the match, but they had then had a game on the following weekend whereas in 2012 the competing nations, apart from Ireland and France who were fulfilling their postponed fixture in Paris, had an extra week to prepare. Some players went into the centre of the capital, expected by the management to celebrate their achievement, but not to excess, and be back at the squad hotel in Richmond at a reasonable time. The players had been together for more than a month and Gatland appreciated that he had to let some steam out of the pressure cooker. 'There were a few people feeling a bit dusty this morning, including me,' said the centre Jonathan Davies, after the squad arrived back in the Vale of Glamorgan at Sunday lunchtime. 'We had a few celebratory beers and you have to let off a bit sometime. You have to make sure you behave and not cause any trouble. You are representing your nation and you know you have to live up to that.'

The victory over England had taken Wales two points clear of England and France at the top of the table, although Les Bleus had their game in hand against Ireland to play the following weekend. Wales's final two matches were at home, starting with Italy, who had never won in Cardiff, although they did leave the Millennium Stadium with a draw in 2006. The words grand and slam were being freely used in print, on the air and in chat rooms, but most of the Wales players, like Sam Warburton, were supporters of clubs in football's Premiership and were only too aware that it had been a season of surprise results, such as Blackburn Rovers, bottom of the table at the time, defeating Manchester United at Old Trafford, while Swansea City had defeated Arsenal at the Liberty Stadium and the day after Wales won the grand slam were to gun down the then leaders Manchester City.

'You cannot look further ahead than Italy,' said Jonathan Davies. 'They are always strong and physical and we have to be in the right frame of mind. If we take victory for granted, it will be a really tight game. We cannot think of what might happen on the last weekend until we get there.' Davies reflected on what he described as the greatest day of his career and the reverse psychology employed by England in the countdown to the game. 'I kept screaming triple crown after the final whistle and it was just an honour to be part of everything. England built us up, which we would normally do to them to try and catch them cold. We knew it would be a very tough game and that they would be very physical. They had a real edge about them and we just about coped. We were expected to win convincingly, but we knew it would be a much closer affair. Tuilagi and Barritt were very physical and also good with ball in hand. People might have thought they had the better of us in midfield but I felt we managed to contain them quite well. Tuilagi was a threat all game but we won and that was what mattered. It was not a great performance by us on the whole, but the sign of a good team is that they can win when not playing well. We have had two massive results in Dublin and Twickenham and we have a huge belief as a squad in our ability. We know what we are able to achieve and we have high expectations.'

Davies played the second half with his Scarlets colleague Scott Williams as his midfield partner, the one winning the match with his late try and the other saving it with his tackle in the final play of the evening. 'Scott's try was just magic,' said Davies. 'I saw him putting the grubber through and when he got the bounce I could not believe it. Neil Jenkins had stressed in the week that there was always space behind and that when we attacked England to look to put the ball through the foot. Scott saw the space Jenks had been referring to and just set off. He had just wrestled the ball off a second row [Courtney Lawes] and that is something we also work on in training, with Shaun Edwards.' As for stopping Strettle: 'I thought he put the ball on his arm and did not apply any downward pressure. I tried to get that across to the referee, but it was not his decision in the end. It was touch and go, and could have gone either way, but in the end it went for us. Our scramble defence had been good all afternoon: we are a tight-knit group and work hard for each other. We want to achieve everything we can and that is reflected in the way we never give up.'

A concern for Wales was discipline. They had received a yellow card at Twickenham for the fourth successive match following Gethin Jenkins against Scotland, Bradley

Davies in Dublin and Leigh Halfpenny in the December friendly against Australia. Added to Warburton's red card in the World Cup semi-final and the costly trips to the sin-bin that had undermined Wales's Six Nations campaigns in 2010 and 2011, it showed how Wales were handicapping themselves. 'We kept the ball really well for the ten minutes Rhys was off the field,' said Davies. 'We are used to playing with 14 men and know now what to do. Not to go further behind for that period was significant: I think England expected to push on in that time and it was a big blow for them. We did not do much with the ball, but we held on to it and kept it away from them. It was a special moment when we were presented with the triple crown and I hope there are a few more days like that in my career. I will never forget it.'

Warburton felt that Wales were living up to the maxim of the golfer Lee Trevino, who once remarked that the harder he practised, the luckier he got. 'Things are going our way and you do need a bit of luck if you want to do well in campaigns,' said the Wales captain. 'In the past we had had a lot of bad luck, something like an intercept pass costing us a game. We work exceptionally hard and any fortune we get we deserve.' Warburton ended the game looking as if he had just gone 12 rounds with a heavyweight boxer. 'I ended up with stitches in my eye and bandages all over me. It is always like that after an England game: it is my fourth and they have all been close. You wake up next morning hardly able to move and they are very similar to South Africa in their physicality. We talked before the game about making history because no Wales team had ever won the triple crown at Twickenham before. Parading the trophy was a reward for the hard work we had put in, but we cannot let up because we have to beat Italy. I know this sounds a bit daft, but I was a little bit disappointed at the final whistle at

Twickenham. I was delighted with the victory and what it meant, but we had not played as well as we had in the first two games. It was not a vintage performance by any means and it was not what we were capable of: we tried to play too much and run the ball back too often. When we did kick, we did not have a good enough chase. The plus side was that we went to a really tough place, played ten minutes of the game with fourteen men and still got a result.'

Wales had not overdosed on fortune in the 2011 World Cup. They had arrived in New Zealand expecting to be involved in a three-way tussle with Samoa and Fiji for second place behind the holders South Africa in their pool, but a few weeks later they were being lauded. Even the former All Blacks captain Colin Meads, not one given to getting carried away, joined in the praise. 'A number of the Welsh players were unknown to us before the start of the tournament,' he said at the end of the group stage. 'The young 10 [Priestland] looks pretty neat and that fella North is going to be one hell of a player. He's tearing the world apart. I think Wales will not only beat Ireland in the quarter-finals but go on to make the final. They are playing good rugby and were unlucky to lose their first match to South Africa by a single point. They then won the rest of their pool games, including a huge one against Samoa, and they have impressed a number of New Zealanders with the way they have been playing. Wales look very good.' Meads had been in Wales earlier in the year, during the Six Nations when Gatland was coming under pressure after a run of eight matches without a win, to promote the World Cup. 'I watched Wales play the All Blacks, South Africa and Australia at the end of last year and they didn't always play that well. They had injury problems, but I thought they only performed against South Africa. Wales are, though, competitive and, on their day, they can beat anyone. Warren is respected back home. He didn't have a great year last season when you look at the start he had with Wales; like all coaches these days he is under pressure to win. I am just surprised that a nation like Wales, with all its history and tradition, does not demand a Welsh coach. Wales have had some brilliant rugby players, true greats of the game, and you would think they would produce some top-class coaches.'

As Roberts stayed up all night after the England game, icing his knee and watching films, he reflected on the World Cup. 'We have pushed on from the tournament, but we are not naïve enough to think we have not had the rub of the green in games to win,' he said. 'We could have easily lost in Ireland, Scotland gave us a very tough challenge at home and we could have lost against England if it wasn't for Scott's heroics and some great defence at the end. It's a fickle game. We could have lost them and people would be talking about Wales hitting a plateau after New Zealand. The World Cup hurt everyone. Moments like that in your career only spur you on to want to achieve bigger and better things, and hopefully there is one around the corner.' Before the start of the Six Nations he had said that Wales's objective was to perform to a higher standard than they had in the World Cup. 'We need to evaluate those displays and raise the bar again. Anything less than that will amount to a disappointing campaign. We could not have a tougher start than Dublin: we played a great game of rugby in the quarter-final against Ireland. We kicked well, we tackled well and we were clever with the ball in hand. We did the basics well and executed the gameplan we came up with to near perfection.'

Wales's first stop in New Zealand was in the capital, Wellington. They were based at Rydges Hotel, where some of the rooms overlooked the Beehive, the executive wing of the New Zealand Parliament buildings, which was designed by a Scottish architect, Sir Basil Spence. A short walk away was the venue for Wales's opening group game against South Africa, Westpac Stadium, or Wellington Regional Stadium as it had been rebranded for the tournament in deference to the various sponsors signed up by the organisers. It was built in 1999 to replace Athletic Park, a crumbling stadium on the outskirts of the city that was deemed to be unsuitable for a professional sport because of its general state of disrepair and its location, and was quickly dubbed the Cake Tin by locals because of its shape. The sea was a punt away and on the quarter-final weekend in October, when Wellington hosted two matches, supporters on cruise ships woke up to find they had docked right outside the stadium.

Wales were the first team to land in Wellington for the World Cup. They were greeted by a crowd of some 200 at the airport on 1 September, most wearing red shirts, some in Welsh costume and most with flags; one supporter was stomping around in a dragon's costume. The Welsh Society in Wellington had planned a series of events, culminating in a Welsh day at Te Papa, the national museum and art gallery of New Zealand that was located in the city centre. They attracted media attention from the outset, both because of Wales's traditional rivalry with New Zealand, even if it had become one-sided, and the presence of Gatland, a coach many felt would be in charge of the All Blacks before the decade was out. The *Dominion Post* gave up one of its main news pages to report the Welsh squad's arrival, even if some of its website readers were not sanguine about the men in red's prospects. 'We will struggle in our group and when we fail to progress, with losses to South Africa and either Fiji or Samoa, there will be the usual wailing and gnashing of teeth but no real progress in Welsh rugby,' posted one. 'The village idiots of world rugby.' Another laconically observed: 'The arrival of Manu Samoa's tackling bags.' Patriotism did prevail with the final comment: 'Go Wales. South Africa will underestimate us and we will beat them!' The general verdict was that Wales would turn out to be half-baked at the Cake Tin.

Gatland had long targeted the opening game, refusing to see the pool as a scrap for second place. South Africa had only once lost a match in the pool stage, against England in 2003, and that was the only occasion when one of the home unions had defeated a major southern hemisphere side before the quarter-finals. The Springboks had finished at the bottom of the 2011 Tri-Nations – the tournament was truncated because of the World Cup – and their one victory came in their final match, against the All Blacks at Port Elizabeth, when the visitors were without a number of their leading players, including Daniel Carter and Richie McCaw. South Africa only managed three tries in the campaign, all scored by hookers, and were heavily defeated in Australia and New Zealand, matches where they fielded largely reserve sides, holding back most of their leading players for the final two rounds, which saw them at home. They lost to Australia in Durban, and even suffered the indignity of being shoved back in the scrum, but the boot of Morne Steyn saw off the All Blacks in a match that was played three weeks before their World Cup encounter with Wales, who, at the same time, were beating Argentina 28–13 in Cardiff with less than half the team that was to begin the challenge for the Webb Ellis Cup. Since winning the series against the 2009 Lions and going on to top the Tri-Nations that year, South Africa had struggled, picking up the wooden spoon in 2010 as well as 2011. There had been a campaign to remove the outspoken Peter de Villiers as head coach and replace him with Jake White, who had been in charge when the Springboks won the 2007 World

Cup. De Villiers was perfect for the media, invariably willing to speak his mind, as he did during the Lions tour when, asked how he could defend a player (Schalk Burger) who had been accused of eye-gouging, he replied that rugby was a rough sport and that anybody who did not like that should buy themselves a tutu and make an appointment at their local ballet school.

De Villiers had kept faith with thirty-something players who been part of the success in 2007 and 2009, the likes of John Smit, Bakkies Botha and Victor Matfield, and thirteen of the twenty-two against Wales had been involved in the final four years before, but there was a concern in South Africa that as a team they were not just over the hill but halfway down the other side. No one questioned that they had a winning mentality and they had in their previous two matches against Wales, both in Cardiff, come from behind to win: they were trailing 20–9 in the second half in November 2010, asserting themselves with two tries in a ten-minute spell of dominance, while five months before, with a largely reserve team, they had rallied from 16–3 down to win 34–31 and leave Gatland cursing the mental fragility that prevented his players from seeing out close Test matches against the top countries. The former Australia outside-half, Michael Lynagh, a World Cup winner in 1991, predicted an early exit for the holders. 'A number of their forwards may be a little aged,' he said. 'A lot of them were involved in the last World Cup: no nation has ever retained the trophy and a lot of the time the reason why is that players hang on too long, hoping to win another one. South Africa did not do well in the Tri-Nations or the Super 15 and I cannot look beyond New Zealand when it comes to who will lift the trophy.'

Gatland had been in bullish mood on the day Wales left for New Zealand. 'We are pretty happy with the preparations,' he said. 'We had two wins and seven tries from our three games in August and we have some youngsters coming through; we have to be excited about going to New Zealand and we will do so with confidence after beating England and Argentina. What has been important for me is to have had the players together for the last couple of months: we have been able to work on a lot of specifics, which you cannot do before autumn Tests and the Six Nations. It has made a big difference to us and we are in good shape.' He was then asked whether, given that South Africa had been playing competitive matches in the build-up while Wales had been involved with friendlies, it would have been better to have faced the Springboks further into the tournament. 'It is hugely positive for us to have South Africa first up,' he replied. 'We have Wayne Barnes refereeing and he is one of the best in the world. I would not want to be playing them last as a decider with referees having quarter-finals to think about: they are under as much pressure to perform as players. We have pushed South Africa close in recent encounters and it is about getting over the line. We know it will be tough, but we can get the victory.'

Gatland said that Wales had emerged stronger for the struggles in 2010. 'We have a number of young players in the squad and they have been incredibly impressive,' he went on. 'It is a healthy environment to be in. They are putting the older players under pressure, forcing them to look at themselves and go up another level. This is the fittest squad I have been involved with and as long as we do not pick up too many key injuries, we have a chance. It is a waste of time getting on the plane unless we believe we can go out there, qualify from the group and perform well. I do not like to think in terms of a minimum target. We want to get to the quarter-finals and take it one step at a time. We believe we are good enough. We cannot look too far ahead of ourselves and we will re-evaluate our goals week to week. The disappointing thing for the coaches in 2007 was that they had put a tight gameplan in place to beat Fiji and for whatever reason the match exploded into a loose affair that played into Fiji's hands. As a result, Gareth Jenkins lost his job, but the players were still employed the following week.

'I have been incredibly impressed by the maturity of the players. They are making a call on Twitter – apparently I have an account, but as I don't it is a fake – and they are making sure they are responsible professionally. Some of the guys will have their families over there and players will room together, unlike England. We will be traditional tourists. The players do not always know there is a massive amount of support in Wales wishing them well. You tend only to hear about the pessimists. They are young men with a huge responsibility and if they know that when they put the jersey on people are supporting them, it can give them the extra one or two per cent that makes all the difference. I have seen players in the past ravaged by criticism, some of it brought on by themselves. It does affect them psychologically. It is hard for anyone to take criticism: I have been around longer and can handle it, but it is not always the case for young men in their 20s and the support we had in Cardiff this month was magnificent.'

South Africa were holed up at the Intercontinental Hotel, the swankiest in Wellington. Teams drew lots to decide where they stayed with the hotels, which varied considerably in standard, selected by the organisers long before the start of the tournament. De Villiers was forced onto the defensive by Gatland at his team announcement. He had chosen the most experienced Springbok team in history with a total of 815 caps; it would have been more had not Botha been ruled out by an Achilles tendon injury. Gatland pointed out that South Africa had not only gone for experience but had opted for five forwards on the bench, including an entire front row. 'I think it is fairly obvious how they are going to play the game,' he said. 'They are going to take us on up front and try to dominate us physically. In our past few games against them we have been winning, only for South Africa to get an impact from their bench. We have to be able to match that and one aspect of our warm-up matches was that the replacements made a positive contribution.' De Villiers said Wales would know what was coming. 'It is important to do what you want to do,' he said. 'You have to play to your strengths. We know what we want to achieve in the game and our bench is a big part of that.'

Wales were without five injured Lions. Matthew Rees and Gavin Henson had not made it to New Zealand, Ryan Jones and Stephen Jones were sidelined by calf strains and Gethin Jenkins had not appeared for Wales all year: he had had surgery on a toe and his attempt to return in August was thwarted by a calf problem. Gatland admitted he had taken a gamble in including Jenkins in the squad, but he was not prepared to pass up the prop's experience, especially with Rees missing the trip.

Gatland was right: the match was influenced significantly by the bench. The Springboks were able to bring on experienced internationals in Bismarck du Plessis, Gurthrö Steenkamp, Johann Muller, Butch James and Willem Alberts, who had scored tries as a replacement in three consecutive matches on South Africa's European tour in 2010, starting with Wales. The decisive contribution was made by Francois Hougaard, who came on for Bryan Habana on the hour. Wales, in contrast, had four replacements who had started three Test matches between them: Lloyd Burns, Ryan Bevington, Tavis Knoyle and Scott Williams. Gatland only made one change during the match, Bradley Davies for Alun Wyn Jones in the second row, and it was the one match in the tournament in which Wales were outscored in the final quarter.

Gatland wound up his team announcement by making a prediction. 'There are three definite world-class players at the breakdown in this tournament – David Pocock, Richie McCaw and Heinrich Brussow,' he said. 'I'd rate the guy next to me as in that category as well. A lot of people have not seen Sam Warburton, but he will create an impact after a few games in this tournament.' Warburton was to be named man of the match two days later, after forcing six turnovers, and his performance prompted a warm tribute from the South Africa captain, John Smit. 'He is a pain to play against. He is unbelievable at the breakdown, really busy and difficult to take care of. He will have some really good Test matches for Wales in the future and I am sure he is going to really stand out in this tournament.'

Smit was speaking as the winning captain after Wales had come closer to beating the Springboks than in any of their twelve matches in the fixture since their one, and only, victory against them in 1999. Wales lost 17–16, having conceded a try after just two minutes, when South Africa had confounded their stereotype and run the ball from the kick-off, taking play through phases before Frans Steyn scored from a scrum. Warburton missed a tackle on Jaque Fourie in the build-up, but he started to get on top of Brussow at the breakdown as Wales looked to keep the ball in hand and move South Africa's forwards around. James Hook quickly got Wales going with a penalty and thought he had kicked a second on 14 minutes. The Cake Tin is regarded as one of the most difficult grounds in the world for place-kickers and a week that had started dry and sunny finished with a cold wind blowing. Hook's second penalty was from 40 metres out, to the left of the posts. He kicked it so high that it went over the line of the uprights. He turned away after the kick, thinking it had gone over after fading late from right to left, but the New Zealand touch judge on that side of the posts, Vinny Munro, ruled that it had stayed wide. Wayne Barnes, the referee, had the option of asking the television match official to adjudicate, but Munro told him there was no need. Wales felt afterwards that Barnes should have gone upstairs, but television replays were inconclusive even if, watching the action on the diagonal from where Hook had taken the kick, it did look to have gone through the posts. Hook did add a second nine minutes before the interval, but only after Morne Steyn had extended South Africa's lead and by now the Springboks were without their lineout general, Matfield, who had suffered a hamstring strain.

Wales trailed 10–6 at the interval despite dominating for long periods but within 15 minutes of the restart they were in the lead. Hook landed a third penalty before, with South Africa having long since reverted to their kicking game and Wales enjoying long spells in possession, Roberts's break was taken on by Toby Faletau for Wales's opening try of the tournament. Hook's conversion gave Wales the lead for the first time and then it became a question of nerve and composure as they waited for South Africa's response. It came, but not before Faletau got over the gainline and found Roberts in support. The centre was held up close to the line and Habana came away with the ball. South Africa were ahead on the scoreboard with 15 minutes to go. They kicked a penalty to touch and took play through phases before Hougaard spotted the prop Paul James guarding a ruck and ran around him to touch down under the posts.

Wales had chances to win. Priestland was well wide with a drop goal attempt from twenty metres before the try scorer Hougaard was penalised for holding on, presenting Hook with an angled kick thirty metres out on the right-hand side eight minutes from time. He missed and South Africa closed out the game. 'How South Africa won the game is unclear,' wrote Toby Robson in the following day's *Dominion Post*. 'Even the most ardent Springbok fan will acknowledge this was a bumbling escape rather than a statement of intent. Wales will wonder how blind-side flanker Danny Lydiate and number 8 Toby Faletau had massive matches but still walked away with their shoulders sagging. Equally how the midfield of Jamie Roberts and Jonathan Davies could look so penetrative but not create even one try for the backs. Most of all they will kick themselves long and hard for being so mentally weak as to not finish a job that has required just one more brush stroke for four Tests in a row.'

Mental strength was a theme taken up by Francois Pienaar, South Africa's World Cup winning captain in 1995, who was a television summariser in New Zealand. 'Wales did not have the belief they could win,' he said. 'And until they do believe, they won't win.' Gatland had a different take. 'We were not clinical enough,' he said, 'but I am immensely proud of the players. We enjoyed 60 per cent of the possession and territory against South Africa and we took a massive step as a team, but it is about finishing on top on the scoreboard and we did not.' Lydiate stressed that the question of Wales's mental hardness would be answered in their next game, against Samoa. 'I am devastated by this defeat,' he said. 'We felt good coming into the game and believed we could win it. We did not take our chances and made silly errors. We keep saying the same thing all the time that you cannot do that at this level and we keep doing it. We should have won, but we have next week to turn it around. We will have our heads on and the sign of a good team is how you react to a defeat like this.'

For the encounter with Samoa, Wales moved to

Hamilton, Gatland's birthplace and where he had a house that his wife opened up for travelling Wales supporters. The build-up to the game was overshadowed by an accident in the Gleision Colliery, a drift mine in the Swansea Valley, that left four miners dead after being trapped underground following an explosion. It was the worst mining disaster in Wales for three decades. 'As Welshmen we have been brought up on tales of mining tragedies,' wrote Alun Wyn Jones in his book published after the tournament, *World Cup Year*. 'We all thought those days were long gone, but sadly that is no longer the case. As a squad we were all devastated by the news and could not stop thinking of the consequences for the families involved and the community in the Swansea Valley.' After Wales had beaten Samoa, and he had been named the man of the match, Jones noted: 'It was a weekend where events back home weren't too far from our minds. Sam Warburton dedicated our victory to the memory of the four miners, David Powell, Phillip Hill, Charles Breslin and Garry Jenkins. As a squad we were disappointed that the authorities refused our request for a minute's silence before the kick-off.'

Jones described the Samoa match as win or bust. When the islanders defeated Wales in Cardiff in the 1991 World Cup, a time when they were known as Western Samoa, it was one of the biggest upsets in the game's history; less so when they repeated it eight years later. By 2012, Samoa had players who had made their reputations in England and France, such as Alesana Tuilagi, Sailosi Tagicakibau, Seilala Mapusua, Census Johnston and Eliota Fuimaono-Sapolu. Wales had beaten Samoa 17–13 in Cardiff in 2009, but the islanders had had little preparation time. They had been together for weeks before the start of the World Cup and it was going to be a game that was as physically demanding as the one the week before.

The score at half-time was the same as it had been at Wellington, 10–6 against Wales. The prop Anthony Perenise rumbled over for a try after the flanker Maurie Fa'asavalu's claims for one had been turned down. Gatland was left to contemplate the most significant half-time talk of his career with Wales: defeat would have left Wales with little chance of making the last eight and would have put the WRU under pressure to exercise the exit strategy it had given itself in the coach's contract. He had lost Lydiate with an ankle injury after nine minutes and Hook did not come out for the second half because of a shoulder problem. There was more at stake for Gatland than there was for the players because he stood to lose his job, but he did not rant and rave, pointing out that they needed to start playing more for territory, reducing the risk of turnovers, and wait for their superior conditioning to kick in. Halfpenny, the replacement for Hook, set up a try for Shane Williams after Priestland had kicked two penalties, and Wales were home 17–10, succeeding where they would probably have failed a year before.

'We knew it was a must-win game,' said Gatland. 'It was all about the result, not the performance, even if there is a lot we have to improve on. You have to give Samoa credit. They worked really hard at the breakdown and made it tough. A few years ago, or even 12 months, we might not have won that game. Our whole World Cup was about going out in that second half and digging deep. And the players did that. They were under pressure and they responded. The longer the game went on, the stronger and fitter we looked. We've worked really hard the last few months and you've got to show people how much it means to us to get out of this and get a win on the board. The bench made an impact and it was good to see Gethin Jenkins back.'

The home element of the crowd was divided in its

support of the two teams and the scheduling worked for Wales, who played both Samoa and Fiji in Hamilton; but for the presence of the local hero Gatland, most of the neutrals would have cheered on the islanders. 'The atmosphere was electric,' said Gatland. 'There was initially a bit of trepidation about playing here, but I think we got a lot of supporters and admirers from how we played against South Africa last week. Our destiny is in our own hands now. We have to beat Namibia and Fiji.'

One result the previous day had changed what lay ahead of Wales: Ireland's victory over Australia. Instead of contemplating a quarter-final against the Wallabies, which South Africa could look forward to, Gatland was left to anticipate Ireland in the last eight, dulling slightly the disappointment of losing to the Springboks. 'Ireland's victory, ironically, potentially favours us going forward in the competition,' he said. 'It could be Ireland in the quarter-final with England or France in the semi-final, if we win our next two games.' Not that there was any doubt that Wales would defeat the tournament whipping boys Namibia in New Plymouth. The Namibians were largely made up of part-timers, but the schedule had them playing their four group matches in sixteen days compared to South Africa's nineteen and Wales's twenty-one. They lost to South Africa 87–0 and 81–7 to Wales, the latter's 11 tries including one from Gethin Jenkins from 25 metres in a match that marked the only appearances in the tournament of Aled Brew, Ken Owens, Craig Mitchell and Ryan Bevington. Six days later, Wales confirmed their place in the quarter-finals with a 66–0 demolition of demoralised Fiji at a wet Waikato Stadium. All of the three-quarters scored tries in Wales's best attacking display, with North taking some stopping, but they also defended with zeal as Fiji, quarter-finalists in 2007, were awarded a raft of penalties in the final quarter and protected their line to gain a measure of redress after the Fijians' draw at the Millennium Stadium ten months before and the defeat at Nantes in the last World Cup. A few hours after Wales had left the ground, the group stage concluded in Dunedin, where Ireland pulled ahead of Italy in the second half to set up a date with Wales and their former coach, Gatland.

'We knew this would be a tough pool and coming out of it does set you up for the quarter-finals and maybe a bit further, but it is one step at a time,' said Gatland. 'We have to build on what we have accomplished.' Wales had conceded seven points in the second half of their last three matches in the pool, a breakaway try scored by Namibia, and none in the final quarter. 'We said before the Fiji game that we were too fit, too big and hopefully too smart. There is no greater motivation than playing in the quarter-final of a World Cup: win that and you are here until the end of the tournament.' Not quite, as Wales were to find themselves flying home the day before the final between New Zealand and France, but a team that had come to dread World Cups since reaching the semi-final in the inaugural tournament 24 years before was leaving on a high. Coincidentally, the last four in the 1987 tournament, which was also held in New Zealand, were the All Blacks, Australia, France and Wales: the one difference was that it had been a north–south split in the semi-finals then while in 2012 the hemispheres stayed apart until the final.

Wales had captured imaginations in New Zealand because they seemed to defy the stereotype of kicking-obsessed, dull-witted and conservative northern sides. They were young, a model of behaviour, unlike England, and they were box office, talked about by New Zealanders on the streets and in bars and cafes. They were the second favourite team of many, as the letters pages in newspapers in Auckland, Wellington and Christchurch showed. 'Crikey, we are in the semi-final of a World Cup,' said

Ryan Jones, who had been on the verge of going home after suffering the recurrence of his calf strain. The victory against Ireland, another game that saw opponents fail to score against Wales in the last quarter, came at a cost: Gatland only brought on two replacements in Wellington and they were both enforced with Luke Charteris replaced at half-time and Priestland suffering a shoulder injury three minutes from time. Wales's fitness allowed Gatland to keep his players unless they were performing poorly, which no one was.

'Wales were impressive,' said the former New Zealand scrum-half Justin Marshall, who spent a couple of seasons in Wales with Ospreys after retiring from international rugby. 'They could have been undone by their inexperience against Ireland had the game got tight, but it didn't. They were ruthless taking points and were tenacious and aggressive in defence. They have players who, because they have not been involved in Test match rugby for long, don't have any fear of failure in their system. Guys like North, Jonathan Davies and Priestland are taking opportunities on the back of more experienced players like Shane Williams and Jamie Roberts. Warburton and Faletau are belying their greenness and playing with composure, a solid gameplan and belief. There have been suggestions that Warren Gatland has his team playing like the All Blacks, but I do not buy that. They don't have the same tempo, particularly in the forwards. They are uncompromising and brutal, but they don't off-load a lot, which is a strength of New Zealand. The Welsh forwards aren't at that skill level. Also their play is very direct. They are not looking to use footwork and speed to outflank; they're basically running at and through defenders. New Zealand play a more manipulative style and are not as confrontational as Wales, who have the ability to get to the final and win.'

The Welsh Grand Slam 2012

France were the jokers, or wild cards, of the 2011 World Cup. The old cliché was that you never knew which France would turn up for a match, the one filled with flair, the one filled with aggression that sometimes flopped on the wrong side of the laws or the one that lacked interest. They were all three rolled into one at times in New Zealand, faltering against Canada and Japan, starting in a rush against the All Blacks before stopping as if there had been a power cut and then losing to Tonga at the end of the group stage. They lost two matches yet made the last eight because Tonga had blown a lead against Canada. They were up against their tournament nemesis, England, in the quarter-final in Auckland, but the men in white were a team in desperate need of home comforts and France suffered little anxiety in winning 19–12 to set up a first meeting with Wales in the World Cup.

Wales's other semi-final appearance had been a 49–6 blowout against the All Blacks, but there was no suggestion of another one-sided encounter. In an interview in the semi-final match programme, Gatland said, 'I know the other rugby nations take us seriously as opponents who can play excellent rugby.' He spoke about his confidence in the team, praising the young players' fearlessness, and discussed his high hopes for the future.

The Welsh Rugby Union decided to show the match live on the big screens at the Millennium Stadium. There was a bigger crowd at Wales's ground than there was at Eden Park, some 65,000 compared to less than 59,000. The WRU initially thought that 25,000 would turn up, given the 9 a.m. kick-off British time, but it underestimated the interest. 'The buzz that is coming back is absolutely extraordinary,' said the Union's chief executive, Roger Lewis. 'Everyone wants to be a part of it and we have been working on how they can do that. The television ratings in Wales have gone off the scale. We have been getting shares of 80–90 per cent and we have heard from the national grid that there have been surges in the morning because people are putting the kettle on for a cup of tea.' Supporters were asked to wear their Wales jerseys to work on the day before the semi-final. Fans booked late flights to New Zealand and found there were hotel rooms to spare, some vacated by England and South Africa supporters who had expected their teams to stay beyond the quarter-finals.

Kiwis were rooting for Wales and some wanted Gatland to succeed Graham Henry as the New Zealand coach. 'We have a rock solid contract with Warren,' said Lewis. 'We have invested hugely in him, we've committed hugely to him and he's committed hugely to us: his wife and kids are thousands of miles away. The next four years are going to be so exciting for us. I've spent 30 years working in the media, record business and television. When your stars take off, you've got to make sure you are contractually sorted and we are. Warren is our producer-director, our stars are our players and you've got to secure the services of them.' Asked what he would do if Gatland asked to be released from his contract so that he could coach the All Blacks, Lewis answered: 'It has not crossed my mind that such a scenario could occur because we are all in such a good place and everything is buttoned down. You are then into the complexities of contracts and the financial implications that go with them.'

After the tournament, the International Rugby Board said that Wales had been the best-behaved team, a contrast to previous excursions. 'Before we flew out, we talked about wanting to be one of the best teams off the field as well as on it,' said the team manager Alan Phillips in *The Times*. 'What is most important is that we sell Wales when we are travelling. You will not get me laughing about what has happened with England. It is crap to deal with and there is no need for it. But you have to have that pain, unfortunately, and come through the other side for the boys to say: "Hang on, this is not acceptable." Martin Johnson has trusted people and this is what happens when you have a couple of idiots in the team. They don't realise what damage they are doing. When somebody from England was fined or there was bad publicity, we put up the newspaper cutting on our team notice board. I wanted the players to be aware of the pitfalls, especially when stuff was caught on film. In all the problems teams have, there is one common denominator: drink. You try to educate people. Players now have a culture of drinking shorts: they slam them down and then lose it. I am chuffed to bits that our players have made such an impression in New Zealand. If that does not lift you, nothing will. It shows we have been doing something right and I pinch myself every day. This team has gained so much respect for Wales in a short space of time.'

There was even more respect for Wales after the semi-final. They lost 9–8, but played the final 61 minutes with 14 men after Warburton's dismissal and, already without the injured Priestland and Charteris, had to contend with the early loss of Adam Jones with a thigh injury. Wales started the tournament by paying for missed kicks and they were knocked out after landing one out of five attempts against France. Hook kicked one penalty but missed two others, slipping once as his right foot addressed the ball. Stephen Jones hit the post with a conversion after Mike Phillips, who had scored one of the tries of the tournament against Ireland, got through the challenge of the second row Pascal Papé. There were 22 minutes to go and Wales were a point behind. Halfpenny was centimetres short with a long-range penalty and Wales spent the final minutes trying to manoeuvre Jones into position for a drop goal but 20 phases came to nothing. Wales showed all the adventure as France used their one-man advantage by not making mistakes, but with Roberts packing down at flanker in attacking scrums, they sacrificed their most forceful runner from midfield.

'I felt our destiny of having a chance of making the final was taken away by the red card,' said Gatland an hour after the final whistle. 'It probably warranted a yellow card. The thing that surprised me was that the reaction of the referee Alain Rolland was an instant one. I thought an experienced official would have taken a minute and brought in his touch judges. They would have had a chance to look at the screen, see the replay and perhaps make a cool judgement. The red card came out of the blue and it ruined the semi-final, but I could not be more proud of the players. What they did in pushing France so close was absolutely courageous. I just feel hollow. There is no discredit to France because they did not make the decision to send off Sam. They are in the final. I just hope they play a bit more rugby than they did tonight.' Gatland caused a stir a few days later when he said that he had considered getting a prop to feign injury after Warburton had been sent off so that, with Adam Jones having already been replaced, scrums would become uncontested. 'We talked about it in the coaches' box but I made the decision that, morally, it would not have been right,' said Gatland. 'It would not have been in the spirit of the game.'

Warburton was suspended for three weeks, ruling him out of the play-off against Australia, who lost to the All Blacks in the other semi-final, the following Friday. The disciplinary panel was impressed first by how Warburton reacted to the decision, not disputing it with Rolland, but walking towards the main stand where his parents were sitting, and second by his candour at the hearing where he did not attempt to make excuses or resort to legalese.

His reaction helped tame some of the hostility generated in Wales, and elsewhere, towards Rolland. 'Sam Warburton is a rare player,' said one IRB official. 'He reacts to success and disappointment in the same way and, strange as it may seem to say about a player who was sent off in a semi-final, he has been a credit to his country, to the World Cup and to the game of rugby. I wish there were more like him.'

The play-off was a match too far for Wales with Priestland and Charteris still unavailable, Adam Jones injured, Warburton suspended, with no specialist open-side flanker to replace him, and Alun Wyn Jones rested. Faletau wore the 7 jersey and Pocock bossed the breakdown. Wales lost 21–18, the score made respectable by a late try by Halfpenny, who in three matches had established himself as Wales's leading full-back. Some 15 hours after the final whistle, the squad was at Auckland airport, ready to return home to a rapturous reception. 'The loss to Australia showed how much we missed Rhys at outside-half,' said Gatland. 'He has developed the most as a youngster at 10 this tournament. His vision, calmness and how he made his centres look good should be commended.'

As the Wales squad returned to camp after a few days off following the victory over England in the 2012 Six Nations, Priestland was concerned that he would struggle to retain his place in the team after his Twickenham trauma. 'It was definitely my poorest performance in a Welsh shirt,' he said. 'I was disappointed after the game and it was a bit of a token gesture celebrating with the team when they were lifting the trophy and doing a lap of honour. I just wanted to get in the changing-room and clear my head. My decision-making wasn't what I'd expect it to be. I was pretty annoyed and I spoke to the coaches straight after the match. They reminded me that everyone had bad games and that you had to learn from them. If I get another chance, I will try to repay the faith. At the time it was not much consolation, but I hope it will make me a better and stronger person and I am already looking forward to the challenge of whoever I am playing against next, whether it is for the Scarlets or Wales. I do not feel pressure because I am wearing the outside-half jersey that means so much in Wales: the only pressure I feel is that I put on myself. You have to justify the faith that has been shown in you by the coaches. I felt down, although not to the same extent, after the game against South Africa in the World Cup because I missed a drop goal at the end. I was thankful to remain on the field at Twickenham and that I was there when we won the triple crown. England did well, they slowed a lot of our ball down and made it very hard for us to play. We have to give them credit, but that's the worst we've played in this tournament: the one positive is we still won. It was one of the biggest challenges we have faced as a squad and we came through.'

There were two ever-presents in the Wales team who had not been involved in the World Cup, Cuthbert and Ian Evans, the twenty-seven-year-old second row who had come through three years of injury torment. A combination of knee, ankle and chest injuries looked to have ended his international career at 16 caps. 'I made it my goal to wear the Wales jersey again,' he said. 'There were some massive low points: I had to start at the bottom of the ladder and work my way back up. It was a slow process. I never questioned my future. If I was that unhappy being injured, the answer was getting back on the pitch. Playing is what puts a smile on my face. I started back with the Ospreys, generated some momentum and things started to fall into place. I played in all except one of the games in 2008, but this time I am more of a part of it and I am a better player than I was then, more mature and more confident. The public are getting carried away with thoughts of the grand slam, but our focus is Italy: we have to turn up, do a job on them and set ourselves up for France. We are learning to close off games. I am sure there were people who thought we would lose to Ireland and England once we went behind, but we stuck in there and drew on the spirit that exists within the squad. In years gone by, we might not have come back to win.'

Gatland again made changes at forward. Warburton suffered a knee ligament injury at Twickenham and was replaced by Tipuric while Matthew Rees, who had recovered from injury, replaced Owens in the front row for his first appearance since leading the side against France in the 2011 Six Nations. Charteris, whose return meant that Wales's number of players who had qualified for England rose to eight (he was born in Camborne), was recalled to the bench, along with Hook, and Gethin Jenkins was made captain, anxious to break his duck with the armband after leading the side three times, against Australia, twice, and South Africa without success. 'Gethin has taken over as captain during games in this Six Nations and we feel it is the right call for us to make,' said Gatland. 'Matthew has enough to concentrate on in fighting for his place: playing against Italy puts him in contention for selection against France. We are lucky enough to have some strong leaders and characters in the team.' Rees's return meant that the Lions front row of 2009, Jenkins, Rees and Adam Jones, was starting a match together for Wales for only the fourth time since the tour to South Africa.

Italy, who had replaced Nick Mallett as coach with the Frenchman Jacques Brunel after the World Cup, were looking for their first victory of the year. They had been well beaten in France before taking a 15–6 lead against England in Rome after forty-six minutes only to concede a soft try and blow two eminently kickable penalties in the final quarter. They then competed against Ireland in Dublin for the first half before collapsing after the interval and Brunel made seven changes for the visit to Cardiff, including the recall of the wing Mirco Bergamasco. They were expected to be no more than a gentle bend as Wales turned into the final straight and their captain, Sergio Parisse, admitted on the eve of the match that the chances of an away victory were lower than low. 'We beat Wales in 2007 in Rome, but at this moment I can't say that we really can defeat Wales because they are playing fantastic rugby. Going to the Millennium Stadium against this team is probably something impossible for us. We must play the perfect match and every player must have his best game of the tournament to beat Wales, who are, without doubt, the best team in the competition. Perhaps their staff and unconsciously even the players are thinking more about the match against France because it's possible for them to win the grand slam. I think they respect us as a team and they know probably for sure we are not the best side in the Six Nations, but if they don't take the match seriously, we can put them under pressure.'

Wales had yet to lead a match in the 2012 Six Nations at half-time, trailing in Dublin and at Twickenham and drawing against Scotland in Cardiff. They started against Italy as if intent on ensuring victory in the opening 20 minutes. Wales went on the attack immediately and throughout the 80 minutes enjoyed 62 per cent of the possession. The penalty count, though, was 13–13 with the referee George Clancy quick to spot offences by the attacking team at the breakdown. The first three rounds of the tournament saw referees allow attacking sides more latitude after a tackle than for a few years, especially when it came to the held player releasing the ball, but this was not as a result of a directive from the IRB, whose then manager of elite referees, Paddy O'Brien, was not impressed at what he felt was an excessively high tolerance threshold when it came to offences like holding on and sealing off. He made his feelings known and there was a marked change in the last two weekends: Wales complained loud and long about Clancy after the 24–3 victory over Italy, but he had merely set the tone for the weekend. The following day in Paris, England's first attack, which took them to the France line, ended when a penalty was awarded against them at the breakdown. The change in emphasis was not lost on Gatland, who spent the following week tailoring his tactics for France.

Wales scored pretty much half the points they had piled up against Italy in 2008, but, on a sunny, early spring afternoon, 2012 was probably more one-sided. Halfpenny gave Wales the lead with a tenth-minute penalty that Bergamasco quickly cancelled out after Wales had collapsed a scrum. Cuthbert had hardly seen the ball against England, but he was soon involved, collecting Priestland's chip and tripping up after crashing through a tackle. Wales off-loaded more than they had all year, but they also made mistakes: Halfpenny lost control of the ball after being tackled by Parisse, Italy's one world-class player, in a challenge that resembled Warburton's on Tuilagi. Faletau had started the move and he was involved again after Halfpenny's second penalty had restored Wales's lead, bursting into the 22 and slipping the ball to Roberts. Faletau took possession again but Bergamasco was penalised for not releasing the tackler and Halfpenny's kick gave his side a 9–3 lead at the break.

Italy struggled to retain the ball they did win, straining to cope with Warburton's replacement, Tipuric, and it was from a turnover forced by Alun Wyn Jones that Wales scored their first try. He secured the ball near his own 10-metre line after a pass had gone to ground and Wales quickly moved the ball left. Priestland, standing at outside-centre, delayed his pass to Roberts long enough to put Bergamasco in doubt as to whether to cover the midfielder or North on the wing. Roberts sensed his hesitation and cut inside as he reached the halfway line. Italy's full-back Andrea Masi was not in position because he had been part of the attack and there was no one in front of Roberts as he sprinted in for his fifth try for Wales, and his first in the Six Nations. Halfpenny's conversion made it 16–3 and Wales for a few minutes threatened to repeat their second-half demolition of 2008. Tipuric was held up short, Jonathan Davies's long pass to Cuthbert, which was almost half the width of the pitch, would have resulted in a try but for Kris Burton's tackle, Halfpenny was again tackled by Parisse with the line beckoning and Tipuric again went close before, after an eleven-phase move, Clancy penalised Wales at a ruck five metres from their line for going off their feet. Five players were on the ground at the time, three attackers and two defenders, and while Adam Jones had entered the breakdown and gone to ground, he had hindered rather than helped his scrum-half, Phillips, who was scrambling for the ball, by pushing Halfpenny over it. It was a penalty offence, but at the same time Bergamasco had his hands on the ball having gone off his feet and, in the previous rounds, he would have been the player singled out.

The crowd booed and the flow Wales wanted to generate slowed to a trickle. The game was won and they could start thinking about the following week, but they found themselves, for the fifth consecutive match, down to 14 men. Priestland's long kick went forward off Bergamasco in the Italy 22, but Clancy waved play on, thinking the wing had played it with his chest, and Italy sent the ball back downfield. Halfpenny gathered and launched a garryowen. He chased after his kick, which covered some 30 metres and had Parisse waiting for it. The number 8 took a spring into the air and, as he caught the ball, was brushed by Halfpenny, who had his eyes on making the catch. Parisse stayed down injured and Halfpenny was sent to the sin-bin. He had been challenging for the ball rather than tackling an opponent in the air but, as with Warburton in the World Cup semi-final, intent was not a factor. The decision had one benefit: Wales had to make a few tackles, early preparation for France. Clancy further angered the crowd when he disallowed a try by Ryan Jones – correctly because a block by Rhys Webb, the replacement scrum-half who was making his Test debut, on Quintin Geldenhuys had created the space for Roberts to run into Italy's 22. Priestland kicked a penalty in Halfpenny's absence to increase the lead to 16 points before Wales, back up to 15 with Hook coming on as a replacement at full-back, scored their second try with three minutes to go. Gethin Jenkins took a quick penalty just inside Italy's half and passed immediately to Cuthbert. The wing shrugged off the replacement prop Fabio Staibano's tackle and had too much pace for the covering Giulio Toniolatti.

Gatland was more frustrated than pleased. 'You have to give credit to Italy for the way they defended, but was their plan to defend and box-kick and wait for us to make a mistake?' he asked. 'They did not play a lot of rugby and Shaun Edwards said afterwards that it was like a training session because he could not remember anyone missing any tackles. We played some great rugby in the first half, but the man with the whistle did not make it easy for us and was reasonably pedantic. A team that has not much territory and possession should not have a penalty count of 13–13. We were not put under any real pressure apart from when Leigh Halfpenny was sent to the sin-bin. I thought that was a bit harsh because he was jumping for the ball and was not trying to take out the player in the air. It was a big call. The boys are a bit flat in the changing room: they wanted to score some points today and felt frustrated at the breakdown, not being able to recycle quick ball and it turned into a dogfight. This will not be a light week physically. We have to make sure we remind the guys that we have to prepare right for a physical encounter. We are at home and we have got a chance. If we do achieve the grand slam, three in eight years would be pretty special. It won't be difficult for us to get through this week at all. The guys have got their heads on. These young players are just taking these things in their stride.'

The match statistics showed that Wales had 68 per cent of the territory, made 101 more passes than Italy and covered 525 metres with the ball compared to 165. They made seven clean breaks to one, forced 19 missed tackles and visited Italy's 22 on 38 occasions. Fifteen of the 26 penalties Clancy awarded came at the breakdown and all bar three went to the defending side. The longer the game went on, the more Wales, who had failed to score a try in the opening half for the third match in a row, joined Italy in kicking ball from their own half for fear of being penalised after a tackle. Bergamasco, who played for Racing Metro in Paris, was one of the few in Cardiff who did not believe Wales would go on to win the grand slam, dismissing them by saying: 'They are predictable. France have the weapons to beat them.'

It was not just grand slam week for Wales: they were going to meet France for the first time since the World Cup semi-final. 'It is a repeat of that day,' said Roberts. 'That defeat hurt and the memory of it will drive us on.' Roberts was cited by some commentators as evidence that Wales had become one-dimensional behind, never mind that Wales's nine tries had all been scored by three-quarters. It was not a view shared by Rhys Williams, a full-back and wing who was part of the 2005 grand slam. 'The back line has danger everywhere and it is good to see the wings coming in field and working hard,' he said on BBC Wales's *Scrum V* after the victory over Italy. 'This side is the best in Europe, one that is going places: it is on the verge of what could be called another golden era. Not many Welsh teams in the past have achieved three grand slams in eight years and we should embrace the fact that we are going into games as favourites. The players will be totally focused this week. They are aware that a grand slam has been on the cards since the final whistle went at Twickenham. We were exactly the same eight years ago when we won in France [in the third round], knowing that something special lay ahead. The atmosphere on Saturday was electric and the crowd will have a part to play against France.'

6

Dan's Inferno

Pick up the pieces you see before you,
Don't let your weaknesses destroy you.
You know wherever you go the world will follow,
So let your reasons be true to you.

Cat Stevens (Yusuf Islam)

FIVE DAYS AFTER WALES DEFEATED FRANCE IN 2012
to win the grand slam, Dan Lydiate was named man of
the tournament after a poll of rugby followers. The shortlist
they had been asked to choose contained the names of
players who had won man-of-the-match awards in the
first four rounds. That Jonathan Sexton finished second,
with every respect to the Ireland outside-half, showed the
system was not necessarily a reflection of the players who
had been most influential in the tournament. There was,
though, little dispute about the winner. Dan Lydiate, as
he showed against France when he was again named the
man of the match, was a worthy recipient, a selfless wing
forward whose tenacity and refusal to leave anything on
the field characterised Wales's tournament. They were not
as flashy as they had been in past years, they did not take
gratuitous risks and they were not as free-scoring as they
had been in the 2005 and 2008 grand slam campaigns,

161

but they were more mature, more calculated, more aware and more single-minded. Winners never have to worry about justifying their tactics; Wales, as was the case in the 1970s, recognised that sport was the art of the probable.

Wales had beaten France by six points to win the grand slam in 1976 and by nine points in repeating the feat against the same opponents two years later. The margin in 2012 lay somewhere in between, a converted try, scored by Alex Cuthbert and fashioned by Lydiate. France mounted their first menacing attack on 19 minutes, forcing their way into Wales's 22. Lydiate tackled the centre Florian Fritz and Wales were awarded a penalty at the subsequent breakdown. Rhys Priestland kicked to halfway and Lydiate won the lineout. The ball was kicked to France and passed to their captain, Thierry Dusautoir, the International Rugby Board player of the year and the one constant in an erratic side. He was tackled by Lydiate and then robbed of the ball by Alun Wyn Jones. Lydiate then got up to play scrum-half, passed to Priestland outside him and Cuthbert had forty metres to go to the line, evading three tacklers as he ran towards destiny.

Back in October 2007, Lydiate did not know whether he would walk again, never mind play rugby, be capped for Wales or take part in a grand slam campaign. He played that month, two months shy of his 20th birthday, for Newport Gwent Dragons in a Heineken Cup group match against Perpignan at Stade Aimé Giral. The match was 15 minutes old when Lydiate made a tackle and fell to the floor. As he sat up, someone landed on the top of his head, which snapped forward. He heard a crack. 'There was a burning sensation in my arms and legs and the feeling was coming and going,' he said. 'I knew it was bad. I wasn't knocked unconscious or anything like that. I remember exactly how it happened and lying there thinking it was not good. It was a pretty scary time: I would not want anyone to have to go through that. The medical people were scared to move me at first, but they took all the necessary precautions and I couldn't fault them.' He had ruptured every ligament in his neck, suffered a broken vertebra and crushed a disc. He was taken to hospital and, after a few days, flown back to Wales in an air-ambulance for an operation he needed to remove the threat of paralysis. He had to first sign a consent form saying that he understood that if anything went wrong he could be in a wheelchair for life. 'They took a bone graft from my hip, put a plate into my neck and basically screwed me back together,' he said in an interview in *The Independent* in 2011. 'And when I woke up the first thing I did was wiggle my toes. I thought "happy days". I was very lucky, because all my training, lifting weights and that, had given me bigger neck muscles than the average Joe. That's what saved me.' It was nearly a year before he played again. 'At first, I didn't know if I would walk or whatever, but it was established I was going to be fine. The next question was whether I would be able to play again. Once I had the operation, they said there was no reason why I couldn't. You just start building from there. When you suffer a serious injury, you look at life in a different perspective. I am just glad I came through it.'

Lydiate was born in Salford. His father, John, was also born in the city and his mother, Lynne, hailed from mid Wales. When he was four, the family moved to a farm in Llandrindod Wells, where Lydiate went to recuperate after his neck injury. 'My father's supportive of me but he's an England fan,' Lydiate told the *South Wales Argus* in 2009, 'but because I am involved I think he would rather Wales win the Six Nations; blood is thicker than water. He did not become interested in rugby until my brother Jack and I started playing the game. He was a football fan in his youth and still supports Manchester United. Coming from where he did, he followed rugby league. It's probably the same for dads the world over: if your son is playing you support them, so there is no dilemma there for him at all really.'

Three days after Wales had won the 2012 grand slam, Lydiate was at Cardiff City Stadium, taking part in a media day organised by the four Welsh regions along with all the other Wales-based players in the Wales squad. Word had leaked out that he had been voted the man of the tournament and the shy 24 year old struggled to take it all in. 'I am quite shocked. It is a massive honour and I did not expect it at all. I did not think it could top winning a grand slam but it is the icing for me and my family. I looked at the names of the players who had won the award before, such as Brian O'Driscoll and Shane Williams, legends of the game, and my name going alongside them did not seem right in my own head. I am so happy. Rugby is about having a mixed bunch of players and that's what makes it so good. You have the old heads watching it in the pub who see the dark arts while the younger people, like the girls who watch, see the backs scoring the tries. I think I would rather have a few more girls saying what a player I am! I wish I could score a few tries, but it is a team effort and you do what you can do to help the performance. Everyone has their jobs to do and I seem to find myself making tackles. You cannot always have the ball in your hands. The way I play at 6 is different to the way, for example, Tom Croft does. I am not saying my way is the right way, it is just what player you are and it is a question of balance in the back row. Toby Faletau is a massive carrier and Sam scavenges the ball. I do more of the tackling. We complement each other.'

Lydiate said he had been worried for his place after missing the opening match in Dublin. 'Ryan Jones played at 6 against Ireland and I thought he would get the man-of-the-match award that game; he was outstanding all championship. I was nervous for my spot and having such strength in depth keeps you on your toes; you have to push yourself harder. Luke Charteris had a hell of a World Cup, picked up an injury and Ian Evans came in and had a stormer. There is so much strength in depth you cannot afford to get injured, but if you do not pick up bumps and bruises it means you are not doing your job properly. All through the squad, we have players competing for places.'

Three weeks before the start of the 2012 Six Nations, Lydiate returned to Perpignan for the first time since he had suffered his neck injury there. He had for a few years forgotten about the incident, but the memory returned when he arrived at Stade Aimé Giral, where the Dragons were playing Perpignan in the Amlin Challenge Cup. 'Human nature means you try not to remember the bad times, just the good ones,' he said. 'When I returned from the injury, I was more tentative in my tackling, but once you start making them, you progress and build year on year. The only time I did worry about it was when I went back to Perpignan in January. I had not thought about it for a while and I had a few demons in my head before the game. When I got through the match, it meant I could put the incident to bed.'

The player Lydiate most admired when he was growing up was Richard Hill, the England and Lions flanker. 'I liked the way he was, the way other members of the team spoke about him. He never got the glory, but he was such a vital cog. I admired that. If I model myself on one player, it's definitely Richard Hill. I'd love to find the same qualities he had.' Sam Warburton had long lauded Lydiate, saying that he was the team's unsung hero, and Shaun Edwards compared the Dragon to the player's role model. 'I thought Dan was our best player in the autumn international series,' said Edwards before the start of the 2011 Six Nations. 'The thing about him is he actually doesn't catch your eye, which is what a good number 6 should be like. If you remember Richard Hill when he was playing for England, you didn't see much of him during the game. But then you watched it back on tape and all the little bits that put the team together he was doing, like his tackling and cleaning the rucks at the right time. That is what Dan was all about in the November internationals. His defensive work rate was excellent and his cleaning-out and carrying were all part of what you want from your number 6. It is all about the cement that keeps your team together.' After the grand slam, he was as full of praise for Lydiate, saying: 'If it was up to me, he'd be man of the match in every game. His attitude, his physical prowess – he's a big man, as heavy as some props – his pace and his tackling ability are second to none. He's also a joy to coach and the kind of lovely lad you'd be proud to have as your son.'

There was another player Lydiate resembled, both in his selfless play and in his humility. Dai Morris made his debut for Wales against France in 1967, along with Gareth Edwards, and went on to win 35 caps. He made his first two appearances at number 8, but then moved to blind-side flanker and remained there for the rest of his international career, which ended in 1974. He was known as 'Shadow', a forward who would materialise when danger threatened and snuff it out. 'He won a place in the affection of his countrymen that was as unsurpassed as it will prove undying for all those who saw his unrelenting, tireless cover and support,' wrote David Smith and Gareth Williams in their history of the Welsh Rugby Union, *Fields of Praise*. 'The slow-burning ferocity of his play was etched in the hewn-out face of the welder from Tower Colliery.'

Morris was part of the 1971 grand slam team, forming

a back-row partnership with John Taylor and Mervyn Davies that spanned 17 Test matches between 1969 and 1973. The build-up to the 2012 match against France was overshadowed by the death of Davies on the Thursday before the game. He captained Wales in the 1976 grand slam campaign: three weeks after victory over France in the final round, when he had remained on the field for the second half despite suffering a calf injury, he collapsed while playing for Swansea against Pontypool in a Welsh Cup semi-final on Cardiff RFC's club ground after suffering a brain haemorrhage. He never played again.

'Dai Morris was a truly terrific player,' wrote Davies in his autobiography, *In Strength and Shadow*. 'Whether he was playing for Wales, or his village side Rhigos, he would approach each game in the same way. He was a godsend to have in your corner but in all the time we played together, I think he only ever spoke to me once during a game. We were heading to a defeat against England at Twickenham in 1974 and were defending a scrum on our goal-line. Andy Ripley picked up the ball from the base and went round the pack. Dai was meant to be first up to tackle him, but he barely moved a muscle. By the time I got my hands on Ripley it was too late and he powered over for the score. As we waited for the conversion attempt, Dai wandered over and said: "Merv, you missed your man."

'"What do you mean, Dai? First man round the scrum is yours, second one is mine."

'"What number's on his back, Merv?"

'"Eight."

'"What number's on your back, Merv?"

'"Eight."

'"Your fucking man then."'

A minute's silence was held in tribute to Davies before Wales played France and the home players wore black armbands. Parallels with the 1970s had been made during the week: Wales won three grand slams between 1971 and 1978, and victory over Les Bleus would equal that achievement, but 1978 was almost the end of an era. Wales won the triple crown in 1979, but players like Edwards, Gerald Davies, Phil Bennett, Bobby Windsor, J.J. Williams, Tony Faulkner and Terry Cobner had gone by the start of the new decade. The year 2012 was more like the start of a new age: with the exception of Stephen Jones, whose involvement in the Six Nations had been as an unused replacement at Twickenham, none of the squad would be retiring any time soon. More than that, Wales were stepping into new territory: Gatland had become their first coach who had delivered success a second time after a dip. His predecessors such as Tony Gray, Graham Henry and Mike Ruddock had not survived the slump. Wales had a slight falling-off for two seasons up to 1974, but John Dawes replaced Clive Rowlands as coach and enjoyed four championship titles in five years. Coaches since then had either flopped and been removed or they had enjoyed a strong start and departed after failing to arrest a decline. That was where Gatland stood in 2010 as pressure built on the WRU to let him go back to New Zealand. 'We knew the quality of the man and we were prepared to show publicly the faith we had in him,' said Roger Lewis. 'I took some stick then, and again at the start of the 2011 Six Nations, but never once did I have cause to regret the decision and before the end of the year the clamour was to make sure that we did not lose him to the All Blacks.'

There was at least one parallel to the golden era: Mervyn Davies had been first capped by Wales against Scotland in February 1969 after he had made just six appearances in senior rugby for London Welsh, the same number of outings George North had had for the Scarlets before his international debut at the age of eighteen and only a couple fewer than Cuthbert. Gareth Edwards was 19 when he made his first appearance for Wales in 1967, a year older than Keith Jarrett, who played against England in the final match of that year's Five Nations championship. J.P.R. Williams was 19 when he entered the international stage in 1969, at the same time as Davies. Barry John and Gerald Davies were 21 when they faced the 1966 Australians; the wing John Bevan was just 20 when he emerged in 1971. Gatland was not afraid to blood young players, confident that his training regime would help offset inexperience. North had won his 20th cap against Italy, the youngest player to reach the landmark in the history of international rugby, but he had very rarely looked a novice. Even Barry John needed a settling-in period and a time out spent on reflection.

Lydiate was 21 when he made his debut for Wales as a replacement against Argentina in 2009, 14 months after he had returned from his neck injury. 'I only got to play for ten minutes, but I loved every moment,' he said. 'I could not stop smiling after the game and kept my cap on as long as I could in the evening function because it was a huge honour for me. My family were all at the game and my mum didn't stop crying all day, she still had tears in her eyes on the following day.' He made his first start the following week against Australia at the Millennium Stadium in a 33–12 defeat, described later by Gatland as like a startled rabbit in headlights. 'Dan is a definitely an unsung hero,' the Wales coach said at the end of the 2012 Six Nations. 'There is not a lot flashy about him. He does a lot of the donkey work to make the others look good and you need those type of people. They are the glue that holds everything together. He is probably a little bit in the same mould that Richard Hill was with England when they were going so well. People used to say how important he was to

169

the team. Dan is a great athlete, a top professional, and he is important for us. The man-of-the-tournament award is no less than he deserves after all the hard work and effort he has put into this side; he is tireless on the pitch and the definition of a team player. Dan is someone every youngster coming into the game would do well to look up to and attempt to emulate.'

The likes of Lydiate, Warburton, Jonathan Davies and Halfpenny, blooded by Gatland after the 2008 grand slam, did not have successful starts to their international careers in a team context, but Barry John did not taste success in a Wales jersey until his fifth cap; it was the same with Gerald Davies. Gareth Edwards was on the winning side twice in his first seven appearances for Wales. The 1970s did not just happen: Wales won the triple crown in 1969, but in 1968 they finished one off the bottom with one victory in their four matches and the year before they faced the threat of a whitewash in their final game against England in Cardiff, winning in what became known as Jarrett's match but still finishing at the foot of the table. It was a time when Wales pioneered the coaching revolution, turning training sessions from something that had been ad hoc and frowned on into something, if not scientific, far more organised and structured. It was little compared to what was to come in the professional era, but success then was underpinned by a combination of supreme talent and attitude. Barry John gave the impression of languor and detachment, wearing a nonchalant air, but he was ruthlessly competitive, motivated by winning, not entertaining. He would often bide his time, waiting for the right moment before moving, never more dangerous than when he was quiet; like a serpent coiled up in the sun, he struck when his victims did not expect him to.

Three players in the 1970s played in the three grand slam campaigns that decade, all backs: Gerald Davies,

Gareth Edwards and J.P.R. Williams. Three players were looking to repeat that feat in 2012, all forwards: Gethin Jenkins, Adam Jones and Ryan Jones. 'It is a big chance for us to make history and you have to look forward to it,' said Jenkins. 'There is a massive expectation on us this week and, from my experience in 2005 and 2008, you have to block out everything in the exterior. It is going to be talked up all week and I suppose I have an extra input this week because I have been involved in two grand slam campaigns. You have to make sure that you are right on the day to perform and the preparation will be geared to Saturday. We have come in under the radar to win the last two grand slams, but we have been favourites to win matches this year, and that has not often been the case since I have been involved with Wales.' Like Jenkins, Adam Jones had missed only one of the matches in the three years. 'I had only been playing international rugby for a year in 2005 and I had not come through an academy system,' he said. 'I found the build-up to the final game that year daunting, but the young players in this squad are better able to deal with it. They have come through the system and they will not be getting excited this week. We were preparing for a World Cup semi-final a few months ago, and this is a similar build-up. We lost to France that day by a point after playing for most of the match with 14 men, but this week is not about revenge. As a group, we are more disappointed by our defeat in Paris in the last match of last year's Six Nations. We played poorly and that cannot happen again.'

Ryan Jones had played a central role in 2008, when he was the captain, and 2005, when he played in the final three matches and made a significant impact. In 2012, he was effectively first reserve, starting the opening match against Ireland in place of the injured Lydiate, covering second row against Scotland with Bradley Davies banned and coming off the bench against England and Italy. Gatland had delayed naming his side to face France by 48 hours to Thursday, but Jones looked destined to be a replacement again. Whereas replacements in the 1970s only rarely got onto the field, and then only if a player had been injured and declared unfit to go back on by a doctor, benches were regularly emptied since the laws were changed to allow multiple substitutions. No team in the tournament had a player who made as great an impact from the bench as Jones: England used seven replacements against Wales, but their combined contribution did not equal Jones's that evening.

'This week, I sort of envy the boys who have not experienced a grand slam campaign because, given their naivety, expectation is a wonderful thing to have,' said Jones. 'This campaign is different from 2005 and 2008 in that success in those years was more of a surprise, virtually out of nowhere. This one is more constructed and we went into the Six Nations with expectation and so far we have achieved what we set out to. Everyone has now played in a high-stakes game and what we have is a group of guys who are incredibly level-headed. Attitudes and egos are left at the front door. This is, essentially, just another game and, if you take it in isolation, it is about getting a result on Saturday. I am pleased with my contribution so far and feel that I have added value. Going into the last game, you feel you have helped put the team into this position. I am enjoying it. Don't get me wrong, I would have liked more game-time, but that is the nature of the beast.'

Wales were confident Warburton would be fit to face France. The captain had missed the two previous home games, against Scotland and Italy, because of injury, and he had not got beyond the first quarter in a game against Les Bleus, injured in Paris in the 2011 Six Nations and sent off in the World Cup semi-final. While Wales stressed during the week that competition for places was intense and no one could take his place for granted, Gatland had a clear default position when it came to selection: the team that started the World Cup quarter- and semi-finals. Shane Williams had retired from international rugby; Huw Bennett had suffered an injury that was to end his season; Luke Charteris had returned to the squad the previous week after recovering from surgery. Matthew Rees would have led Wales in the World Cup and, having played against Italy, he was back where he would have been. While the Wales coaches praised Tipuric for his performance against the Azzurri, Warburton was always going to return to the side if fit, just as Lydiate had come back in for Ryan Jones after Dublin and Alun Wyn Jones had then replaced Jones in the second row at Twickenham. When Gatland announced his team to face France, the back division was unchanged, as it had been all tournament, and contained six of the starters in the World Cup knockouts. Warburton returned to lead the side, which meant that Wales had had a different set of forwards every match: six of them had started against Ireland and France in the latter stages of the World Cup, Rees and Ian Evans the exceptions. It was not enough to win a match, as Scott Williams had, or stand out, as Tipuric, Rhys Gill, Ken Owens and Ryan Jones all had. Gatland relied on evidence accumulated from a number of internationals, not one or two, before making a paradigm shift, and two of his leading performers in 2011–12, Priestland and Halfpenny, had been given their opportunities by accident, the former after Stephen Jones's injury at Twickenham before the World Cup and the latter during the tournament when, after Hook suffered shoulder damage, the next in line, Lee Byrne, failed to impress. Warburton's elevation to the captaincy, which had been central in changing the culture (to use a word that had become voguish) of the squad, came after Rees required neck surgery, but it was a move Gatland would probably have made anyway in time.

Two dips in performance against England and Italy did prompt Gatland to warn some players that they had been fortunate to retain their places. 'When Warren announced the team to play France, he was frank with three guys, saying he thought they weren't stepping up to the mark and were lucky to keep the shirt,' wrote Shaun Edwards in his column in *The Guardian*. 'Honesty is very much part of the ethos. Tell a player where he is and there can be no misunderstanding. Tell a player what's expected of him and he is less likely to fall short, which is one of the reasons why we like to set targets for the defence. Look around the squad and there is competition for places everywhere except perhaps one, the number 3 position where Adam Jones is yet to feel the heat of someone else's breath on his neck. He's world class but has to be challenged in other, more subtle ways. Elsewhere, a queue has formed to wear the shirt.' Edwards felt that if Wales did win the grand slam, it would be markedly different from the 2008 success. 'Five years ago, we might have surprised a few people. A new coaching team coming together and producing immediate results. This time around there has been the feeling that, in a country where rugby matters so much to the general feeling of well-being, success has been earned, has been part of a cycle and a process. True, we weren't considered favourites at the start of the tournament. That was France and despite a couple of hiccups they are still a considerable team that could easily upturn the apple cart. They still have the potential to play like the side that should have won the World Cup final in Auckland last autumn, but we are also a team that is built on the foundations laid in New Zealand.'

Wales had been almost as resolute in defence under

Edwards as they had been in 2008, three tries conceded compared to two, with only Ireland scoring against them in the final quarter. 'We demand much more than most teams from our tight five, which is, perhaps, why they have to be – and are – probably the fittest unit around. Saying they are there to do the donkey work is putting it a bit bluntly, but that's precisely what their job is. We don't want backs getting involved in the breakdowns. I can remember a statistic, boasted proudly at the time, that in one England Test Jonny Wilkinson had been involved in helping to clean out, from memory, 15 rucks; well, that's precisely what we don't want. We expect our front five to not only do their jobs at the set-pieces and make their tackles in open play but to be part of the process that creates the mismatches which the attack can exploit. And I don't mean gaps; I mean situations where a Welsh player with a high number on his back is confronted by a low-numbering member of the opposition.

'That's it. It may be fairly pragmatic, but that is how we go about our work. It may be only part of the thinking, and only part of what we are about, but it may help in understanding what has been happening since that last slam in 2008.'

France were under new management in 2012. Philippe Saint-André, who won sixty-nine caps on the wing for Les Bleus in the 1990s, had taken over from the iconoclastic Marc Lievremont, who had spent most of his four years as head coach criticising his players in public. Rarely a day passed in the World Cup without at least one story of French disharmony. Lievremont at times questioned aloud why he had taken the job, but he knew that no matter what happened in New Zealand, he would not be around for the following year's Six Nations; Saint-André had already been appointed. His formative coaching years had been spent in England, where he ended his playing days. He became Gloucester's director of rugby, working with the former Wales captain Kingsley Jones, and the pair then moved to Sale, winning the Premiership in 2006, breaking the domination of Leicester and Wasps. He was far more English than French in his approach, given far more to structure than free-will, and when he moved to free-spending Toulon in 2009 he brought English organisation to the south of France, not least in the acquisition of the outside-half Jonny Wilkinson. Saint-André said he wanted to make the national side more consistent rather than a side that lost to Tonga one week and beat England the next. He enjoyed victory in his first two matches in charge, against Italy and Scotland, but both performances were a patchwork of brilliance and basic ineptitude. France were suspect defensively, but with their third and fourth matches at home to Ireland and England respectively, the pre-tournament favourites were fancied to arrive in Cardiff on the final weekend chasing the grand slam. They turned up chasing their own tails after coming from behind to draw with Ireland and losing to England after Saint-André had shown the same eccentricity in selection as Lievremont. Even though he had two of the leading scrum-halves in Europe to choose from, Morgan Parra and the fit-again Dimitri Yachvili, he plumped for Julien Dupuy against England, partnering him with the prosaic Lionel Beauxis. The pair had played together at half-back for Stade Français, but if the intent was to use them as controlling influences, playing for territory and keeping England on the defensive, the strategy was wrecked after twenty minutes with England scoring two tries from French mistakes.

France arrived in Cardiff with the title beyond them, never mind the grand slam. Saint-André again reshuffled his side, recalling Yachvili and the veteran hooker William Servat, who, along with the flanker Julien Bonnaire, was making his final appearance in international rugby: seven of the pack were in their 30s. The maverick in Saint-André moved Wesley Fofana, who had marked his first four appearances in the blue of France with a try in each of them, from the centre to the wing, bringing the bulkier Florian Fritz into the midfield to deal with Wales's monoliths, North and Roberts especially, behind the scrum. Beauxis remained and signalled his intention in the opening minute when he lined up a drop goal near the halfway and sent the ball skidding along a surface that had been livened up by a downpour minutes before the teams had taken the field.

The roof was open even though the weather had been unsettled all week. Saint-André had refused Wales's request to close it, which was taken as an indication that France intended to play ten-man rugby and put the ball in the air rather than through hands. He said he had made his decision merely because a shut roof would mess up the GPS system he had introduced to track his players during a game and measure their performance. Gatland attacked France's decision during his team announcement, although he had not been averse to using the roof as a weapon. When Wales played Australia at the Millennium Stadium in 2010, they were ravaged by injuries behind. Gatland decided it was not the time to be taking on the Wallabies in a running game and ordered the roof to be kept open. That was an exception: his view was usually that if the weather forecast was poor, the roof should be shut, a contrast to the days of Graham Henry when he made his decision based on the qualities of the opponents Wales were facing, prompting the Australia centre Tim Horan to remark that having the roof open to the elements on a rainy day was tantamount to having a Ferrari but parking it outside rather than in the garage.

'France have requested the roof be open and they have

an old, tough forward pack,' said Gatland. 'It is not going to be a pretty game from their point of view and we have to expect a raw, physical confrontation. If the weather is showery and the roof is open, with the side they have picked I would expect them to be more physical than open. Philippe is being pragmatic with the roof. He wants to get a win. I have coached against him in the past in the Premiership and he is conservative in the way he approaches the game, set-pieces and big, physical players. I do not think he cares too much about the type of rugby they play. His whole focus is trying to win the game. It is the first time I have known France ask for the roof to be open. Maybe as a Welsh union we need to make some representations to the International Rugby Board. It is our stadium and we have the ability to open and close the roof. Perhaps we should be the team that decides that. I would hate to think that if it pours with rain and we have the chance to close the roof the game becomes less open and attractive. We all have a responsibility to the broadcasters and the public and the sport as a whole to make the game as attractive as possible and if that means closing the roof because it is wet, we should be able to do that. But the rules are the rules and if one side wants the roof open, unfortunately it is. I hope that it is not closed on Friday night and then it breaks down and we can't open it!'

Gatland said he would feel more satisfied than he did in 2008 if Wales won the grand slam. 'If we win on Saturday, the success will have come from the last eight months and the build-up to the World Cup and the momentum it has created. It is tough winning a grand slam: you need a bit of luck and then build confidence and momentum. England have only won one Six Nations grand slam and that shows how hard it is to do it. We have given ourselves an opportunity and three players have the chance to make it three slams. What we are excited about is where we are now and we can build on this over the next couple of seasons.' He was asked about the comparisons that were being made in the media with the 1970s. 'You are talking about different eras,' he went on. 'The structures were not the same. A number of the players from that decade are still household legends, not just for what they achieved with Wales but with the Lions in 1971 and 1974. We have a 70 per cent success in the Six Nations since 2008 and that is pretty commendable. What does not make you look so good is that when we play the southern hemisphere teams to improve as a side, we have not been as successful as we would have liked, and that is the next step we have to take.'

When Wales played France for the grand slam in 2008, the second row Ian Gough won his 50th cap, a landmark Rees was to reach on the Saturday when he would lead out the team. He was part of the 2008 squad, starting against Italy and Ireland and coming on as a replacement in the other three matches. A season that had started with a surgeon telling him he would not be able to lead his country in the World Cup held the prospect of a far happier ending. 'As much as it was all doom and gloom at the beginning, I could see light at the end of the tunnel,' he said. 'The neck injury was a bit of a concern when we started preparing for the World Cup, but after seeing the surgeon I was happy there were not going to be any issues after the operation and I would be able to resume playing. And now I am on the verge of winning my 50th cap in front of a full house in Cardiff with the grand slam to go for. You could not ask for a better game to be involved in. The pressure is on us and France will want to come here and spoil the party. We have to make sure we deliver. With the changes France have made up front, they are definitely going to try to come here and bully us. That is one thing we have got to be mindful of. They have picked a front five to try to irritate us and see how we respond. One team that tries to bully you is South Africa, but as far as I am concerned whenever we have played at home I don't think there is any team that has come out on top. As a pack, we've got plenty of experience and hunger. We are relishing the challenge. We were always going to be the favourites for the Six Nations in the eyes of many after the World Cup, and you cannot underestimate how big that tournament was for us as a nation. In the past, we have always come into the Six Nations as underdogs, but this group of players has taken us to the next level. Our fitness means we come through strong at the end of games and we have some young boys in the team who are going to be around for a long time.

'We have come a long way in the last 18 months, and what is important now is that we don't get carried away but keep on building. The big question was whether we would continue what we had started in the World Cup and now it is a matter of growing from here.'

Warburton was fit to lead the side and at the team announcement was prepared for the inevitable question of his previous encounter with Les Bleus when he received a red card. Vincent Clerc, the wing he tip-tackled that day, would not be playing after being injured against England. 'There are much more important things to worry about this weekend than the World Cup semi-final and the fact Clerc is not playing makes no difference,' he said. 'All that matters is that we are ready. I have started against France twice and have yet to make it past the 20-minute mark: I was sent off in the semi-final and was injured in Paris last year. It would be nice to stay on a bit longer and have a good outing against Thierry Dusautoir, the world player of the year and someone I respect highly. I watched the 2005 and 2008 teams win the grand slam and it made me want to play rugby. This will be the biggest game of my career and it cannot come quickly enough.' Warburton then revealed he had been a marked man in recent matches. 'I have felt a target,' he said. 'You feel cheap shots coming in left, right and centre but that is part and parcel of the game, I guess. Maybe it is a compliment, but I don't mind it. I play 7 because I like physicality and confrontation. I played on the wing when I was young but I did not get involved enough. It does not bother me. France have picked a physical pack: happy days.'

News of Mervyn Davies's death broke on the day before the match. The flags at the Millennium Stadium were lowered to half-mast and after Wales's captain's run at the ground that lunchtime, Rob Howley paid tribute to a forward who had revolutionised the role of the number 8, turning it from a position that was seen mainly as defensive into a multi-dimensional one, not that he was ever known to shirk a tackle. 'It's a sad day for Welsh rugby,' he said.

'The players, the management, we all send our sincere condolences to the family. Unfortunately, I never played with him, but from what I'm told he was a colossus. To only lose nine games as a player for Wales, the amount of caps, to play eight Tests for the Lions, he's an icon of world rugby. We can speak frequently of world-class players, but icon and legend belong to Merv the Swerve. The players were told this morning, and it gives us even more motivation for tomorrow on what I hope is going to be a great day for Welsh rugby. It is emotional. I met Mervyn on several occasions when I was Wales captain and he gave me plenty of words of wisdom. He was a very humble man who knew the game inside-out.' There was a parallel with 2008: that season, a member of Davies's 1976 grand slam side, the centre Ray Gravell, had died. His daughters, Gwenan and Manon, were the mascots for the final match of the campaign against France and in their final training session the previous day, the Wales squads had worn red T-shirts sporting Gravell's number and the number he wore on international duty, 13. The weather had been cloudy and dank that day, but the roof was closed.

It was estimated afterwards that some 250,000 fans descended on Cardiff for the final day of the 2012 Six Nations, even though fewer than 75,000 had tickets. Big screens were put up in different parts of the city and pubs reported afterwards that they had come close to running out of beer. A supporters' village was set up in Heath, a couple of miles out of the centre, but many followers stayed at home: the average television viewing figure for the match in Wales was 940,000, 80 per cent of the audience, compared to 30 per cent in the United Kingdom. It was the highest figure for any Five/Six Nations campaign and no programme in Wales had attracted such a large audience in 2012: the next four were Wales's other matches in the Six Nations. The first impression strolling around the streets of the centre of the capital early in the morning was that it was France who were after the grand slam: there seemed to be thousands of blue-shirted figures walking around, trying to make themselves understood in cafes, bars and shops, but gradually the tide turned red. The Wales players travelled to the ground by coach from the Vale of Glamorgan, watching a video that included footage of Warburton's red card in the semi-final as well as clips of action from the previous four matches, tries and big hits. Even those who had been part of previous grand slam campaigns were surprised by the reaction of supporters they passed en route. If in 2005 the prevailing mood among a success-starved rugby nation had been a mixture of nerves and apprehension because it had been twenty-seven years since Wales had last achieved the clean sweep, the atmosphere was more calm and understated three years later, a consequence, perhaps, of Wales's poor World Cup in 2007. In 2012, there was an overwhelming belief that Wales had a team that was not just on the verge of another grand slam but which was good enough to end the years of bust that tended to follow a short boom. The difference was, in a word, expectation.

France had the best record at the Millennium Stadium of any side in the Six Nations. They had suffered one defeat there in the tournament, in 2008. They had only lost in Cardiff, friendlies excluded, three times since 1982 and a series that Wales had dominated initially was tied at 43–43. Wales were looking to achieve the grand slam for the 11th time and they had only three times been denied at the final hurdle, twice by France in 1965 and 1988. It was also the end of a sequence of fixtures, Ireland and England away and France at home, that Wales had only won in a block once since 1978.

Gatland (who a couple of weeks after the 2012 grand slam success broke both his heels in a fall from a ladder at his beach house in New Zealand) used his column in the match programme to observe that the team was in a position to make history. He pointed out that the Welsh national team had not achieved so much since the 1970s and that his players were well aware of how much was at stake in the game. Acknowledging that Wales had had some good fortune in the competition, he said, 'we have also made our own luck'. Clearly extremely proud of his players, he stated that the grand slam was 'no less than [they] deserve' and reasserted his, and the Welsh nation's, faith in the team.

Wales had faith, France hope, but neither side showed charity in what was a full-blooded, slightly old-fashioned contest. At times it resembled American football, a match coming down to a few plays. 'It is not going to be pretty but it is going to be brutal,' said the BBC's summariser

Jonathan Davies as Beauxis prepared to kick off. *The Guardian*'s chief sportswriter Richard Williams had, the previous day, lamented the passing of artistry in Wales's back play. 'Any team wearing the red shirt have a responsibility to live up to a certain ideal,' he wrote. 'Gatland would be unlikely to give that notion much of a hearing. The New Zealander's priority, his obligation, he may say, is to create a side capable of beating the best in the world, and his very effective method has been to assemble a group of large, powerful and conspicuously fit young men whose opponents fear their physical strength. The tries against Italy were characteristic in that neither score required the deployment of the more delicate arts once associated with Welsh backs: the swerve, the sidestep, the jink, the feint, the smuggle, the dummy. They were the product of strength, speed and, most of all, size. No one exemplifies the change of style from guile to grunt more than Priestland, whose functional role in this Welsh side is so far removed from that of the best-loved wearers of the number 10 shirt, rugby's own lyric poets. No doubt he is playing to instructions, but there is so little joy or creativity in what he does that he may as well be working in a tax office, which is not something you would ever say about Gavin Henson. And without those qualities, which traditionally provide a release from daily care, what is the point of Welsh rugby?'

That was being asked in the 1980s and 1990s when Wales showed flair but little else as they stumbled from one record defeat to another. The romantic image of Welsh rugby is distorted: the best teams down the ages, international and club, have been the ones that blend artistry with industry, as Wales had done in 2012, and mix light with shade. After the Lions had left New Zealand in 1971 having won a Test series there for the first, and only, time, the All Blacks' captain Colin Meads mused that they would have been more convincing winners had Barry John kicked less and passed and run more. That was hokum. John shut the door on the All Blacks, having worked out the way to win. Priestland may have been in a different mould from predecessors like John, Phil Bennett, Cliff Morgan and Cliff Jones, but he had craft, as he showed in creating Wales's first try of the tournament against Ireland, a model of outside-half play. Wales, it was true, lacked a second-five, a centre who had experience of playing outside-half and brought a footballing dimension to the midfield, and that meant the burden of kicking and passing long fell largely on Priestland. The Scarlet was, of course, operating in a gameplan but it was his ability to read play quickly, appreciating what was on before he received the ball, that made England target him at Twickenham.

Beauxis, not Priestland, kicked off. The ball, appropriately, given the applause that had broken out before the start in tribute to Mervyn Davies, was taken by the Wales number 8, Faletau. Phillips's clearance prompted Beauxis's attempt at a drop goal and that started a passage of play that was to characterise the match, kicks being returned. Wales had an early lineout and tried to work a similar play to the one that had nearly resulted in a try for North at Twickenham: Phillips slipped the ball to Cuthbert, who had come inside from his wing after Alun Wyn Jones had caught Rees's throw, but Dusautoir was more alert to the threat than England's back row had been and no gain was made. Jonathan Davies made a half-break two phases later and the centre then found space on the left wing only for Fofana to haul him down. He passed in field but Pascal Pape made the intercept and Beauxis cleared. The early Welsh surge got the crowd going, 'Hymns and Arias' ringing out, but France held their nerve, marshalled by the recalled Yachvili. Dusautoir was thwarting Wales with his reading of play, but after he had forced a scrum by preventing release from a maul, France were penalised for an early engagement. The referee was Craig Joubert, who had taken charge of the World Cup final and had the French cursing privately, Yachvili apart, about New Zealand getting the rub of the decisions. He was more laissez-faire in Cardiff, as if trying to coax an open game from two teams committed to minimising mistakes.

The game quickly settled into a pattern. Neither side was prepared to run the ball from its own half unless there was clear space to attack for fear of being penalised at the breakdown. It was the return of aerial ping-pong and Wales were also conscious of France's line speed in defence. There were 88 kicks out of hand in the 80 minutes, but when Wales did force a mistake, Imanol Harinordoquy dropping Priestland's bomb and conceding possession to Warburton, Alun Wyn Jones entered the breakdown on France's 22 off his feet to prevent Dusautoir forcing a turnover and conceded a penalty. France were blown for an early engagement at the second scrum, prompting Mike Phillips to tap and go. He was stopped on the floor but picked himself up and carried on running, only to find Joubert's arm raised against him, having been held in the tackle. There was little continuity in the opening stages, France looking to slow the game down. Les Bleus achieved their first attacking position on ten minutes, moving the ball from a lineout and winning a penalty when, after Lydiate tackled Harinordoquy, Jenkins tussled for the ball off his feet and Yachvili put his side three points ahead.

Roberts's chip gave Wales an attacking lineout and Wales forced a series of drives, but found themselves going backwards. Halfpenny tried to step inside but was nailed by Fritz and took a bang on his knee. Wales were awarded a penalty when Yachvili failed to roll away and Priestland stepped up to take it because Halfpenny was receiving treatment. The kick was from 40 metres wide on the right. The outside-half tried to bring it in from the right but it hit the post and Harinordoquy secured the rebound. The third scrum of the game ended with Jenkins penalised for taking it down: the set-piece had become in the modern game less a means of restarting play than a means of awarding a free-kick or a penalty, but it was Wales who were to profit from the decision even though Yachvili found touch near Wales's 22 and Servat's short throw to Dusautoir presented the hooker with an opportunity to make inroads on the blind-side. France moved the ball quickly left, but Lydiate's tackle on Fritz was followed by a penalty to Wales. Priestland kicked to halfway and, three interventions by Lydiate later, Cuthbert stepped away from Bonnaire and Yoann Maestri, after receiving Priestland's long pass, on his way to the France 22. Clément Poitrenaud stood between the wing and the tryline, but as the full-back braced himself in a crouch for the impact, Cuthbert, using skill rather than strength, stepped inside him for his third try of the tournament.

Halfpenny's conversion put Wales 7–3 in front, a lead they were not to lose. It was an opportunist try: Priestland, appreciating Wales had turnover ball, kept the ball in hand, knowing the line speed of France's defence would not be an issue. He had had the option of slipping a short pass to Ian Evans to come inside on the crash-ball, but the outside-half had spotted that Cuthbert had forwards in front of him and exploited the mismatches. The score hardened France's resolve: Bonnaire hacked on from a Wales lineout but Priestland was the first to reach the ball after it settled under the posts. Beauxis bombed, Wales boomed back. Wales off-loaded for the first time on 26 minutes but still found themselves operating behind the gainline and went back to kicking, not to touch but into

France's 22, looking for a forward lurking there. When Priestland found Poitrenaud, France countered only for Harinordoquy to pass the ball into touch. It was another gruelling, physical slog, but gone were the days when the top teams outmuscled Wales. France looked for cracks but found only concrete. The ball actually emerged from a scrum, so surprising Faletau that he knocked on. France then got the ball from their scrum, but they had been twisted sideways and when Beauxis received a pass he was smashed by Jonathan Davies. The ball went loose, Davies hacked on and, although it was gathered by Alexis Palisson in his own 22, he held on to the ball under Davies's challenge and Halfpenny kicked the penalty from 25 metres to make it 10–3.

Lydiate was making his impact felt, thumping Poitrenaud to the ground after the full-back had caught a Priestland garryowen under pressure. Wales then missed a chance to counter-attack when Roberts dropped a pass from Priestland that was fading as it reached him. Poitrenaud was injured catching another Priestland high kick, Roberts caught his own chip and Wales mounted their final attack of the half, only to turn the ball over. Evans charged down Yachvili's kick and, in the scramble for the ball, Pape strayed off-side to give Halfpenny the opportunity to give Wales a ten-point interval lead with a penalty almost from the same spot from where he had kicked his first; like Priestland he hit the post and again Harinordoquy gathered, the last act of the opening half.

Warburton did not reappear for the second half as his French jinx continued. He suffered nerve damage in his right shoulder in an incident he could not later recall and was to be out of action for six weeks. Jenkins took over the captaincy and Ryan Jones came into the back row, leaving Wales without a specialist open-side to compete against Dusautoir in full flow. Priestland gave Jean-Marcellin

Buttin, Poitrenaud's replacement, an early high ball but it was dealt with securely only for Beauxis to kick loosely downfield. Priestland took possession with the nearest defender 30 metres away. He fed Cuthbert, who ran at the prop David Attoub and away from him, before getting away from Harinordoquy. He found Faletau with a suspiciously forward pass but when Priestland tried a long-range drop goal, it was not much better than Beauxis's. France seemed to be playing not to lose rather than win, but when Yachvili, looking off-side, ran back a kick, Buttin chipped into Wales's 22. The ball bounced over Phillips and Buttin and glanced Halfpenny before being picked up by Gethin Jenkins in an off-side position. Beauxis took the kick from the left-hand side and it was a four-point game.

France started to take play through phases, but after managing three Beauxis had had enough and tried a drop goal from 30 metres. It was better than his first effort, but was well wide. France had the momentum, but Ryan Jones forced a turnover and then thwarted a counter-attack after France had stolen a Wales lineout by stopping Palisson after a smart off-load by Fritz, who then knocked on. Wales had space to exploit, but Dusautoir's tackle on Roberts ended the threat and knocked on. Fofana had his first run of the afternoon, but France lost control of the ball and Gethin Jenkins launched a kick downfield. Back came France, but they were back on the halfway line. Fofana tried to cut inside but was felled by a typically low Lydiate tackle. The wing held on to the ball and Halfpenny stepped up to take the penalty from just inside his own half. It was from close to the same position as the one he missed in the World Cup semi-final, but it was some six metres longer. His kick in Auckland had dipped at the last but this time it landed just short of the dead-ball line. Wales were again a converted try ahead and there were 27 minutes to go.

The Welsh Grand Slam 2012

Scott Williams came on as a blood-bin replacement for Jonathan Davies and François Trinh-Duc was finally deployed by France, though as a replacement for Palisson, not Beauxis, and went to full-back. Les Bleus were showing more intent, having to chase the game, but they were undermined by their handling and conceded another scrum penalty. Wales enjoyed a spell of possession but, without Warburton, they struggled to generate quick ball at the breakdown, an area where both teams had come to realise that Joubert was not disposed to penalise the attacking side. Wales kept the ball for four minutes before Priestland's cut-out pass just inside the France half was missed by Roberts and dropped backwards by Williams. Cuthbert was then caught on the wrong side of a ruck and France had the chance of three points. As Wales prepared for a kick at goal, Beauxis saw Buttin on the left wing and kicked the ball to him. Buttin caught it 35 metres out and sprinted towards the line. Only Priestland and Lydiate had read the danger and desperately tried to get across. The outside-half got there first, six metres from his own line. Buttin stepped inside him, but Priestland, at full stretch, clipped his thighs before Lydiate knocked him backwards. 'I was walking back the same as everyone and I was hoping someone else would get him,' said Lydiate the following week. 'Rhys slowed him up so I could get across. I am not sure I would have got to him otherwise.' One scrum later, after a thumping tackle by Roberts on Aurélien Rougerie, and Wales had a free-kick for France yet again engaging early at a scrum. There were 20 minutes left.

Priestland worked space for Faletau, but Dusautoir was, as ever, alert, and the number 8 found an open door slammed shut in his face. Priestland's chip was fielded by Rougerie under pressure and the ball came to Buttin. A thumping sound could be heard above the murmur of the crowd, the noise of Lydiate hitting an opponent with such force that the ball went forward and Wales had a scrum. Before it could be taken, Gatland brought on three replacements: not only was it unusual for him but two of the changes saw experienced players, Phillips and Rees, making way for rookies who had both won their first caps less than a year before, Lloyd Williams and Owens. The third was Charteris for Alun Wyn Jones. It was a reflection of just how much Wales had put in, but after Wales had been awarded their customary free-kick at the scrum and opted for another, Faletau was caught in possession and France had a penalty to kick to touch.

They opted for a lineout and forced their way towards the Wales line but Dusautoir held on after being tackled by Owens and challenged by Jonathan Davies, who had just returned to the field. Wales were 12 minutes away from the grand slam and there were to be no more speculative passes. Priestland either kicked or passed inside, running down the clock. It was France who had to take risks. North gave France an opportunity when he went off his feet at a static breakdown and Wales were back in their own half. Dusautoir took the lineout and Beauxis made his first telling kick of the afternoon: Halfpenny failed to make the catch and Fritz pounced on the loose ball only to be caught by Lloyd Williams. France moved the ball right and when Harinordoquy took possession, he had the replacement second row Julien Pierre free outside him seven metres from the line because North had made a vain attempt to intercept. The number 8 had no faith in Pierre's pace because he cut inside and was tackled by Roberts. Lloyd Williams then nailed Yachvili, but France were awarded a scrum. Saint-André finally replaced Beauxis and on came Parra. Wales wheeled the scrum ten metres in front of their posts but, with seven minutes left, Dusautoir was content with the three points that the boot of Yachvili served up.

It was now that the endurance work Wales had put themselves through in Poland would tell. Lydiate picked up a loose kick and freed Halfpenny, who broke into French territory. Priestland sent a rolling kick into France's 22, which was fielded by Trinh-Duc, who was tackled into touch, stupidly throwing the ball away even though no Welsh player was trying to take a quick throw, and Halfpenny had a 25-metre penalty to the right of the posts. He took his time and when he made it 16–9, there were four minutes to go. France conceded a penalty from the restart and conceded ten metres for disputing the decision. Priestland found touch beyond the visitors' 10-metre line, but Harinordoquy got in front of Faletau and tapped the ball back. Ryan Jones seized the ball ahead of Dusautoir and Wales worked a series of pick-and-gos as Priestland got into position for a drop goal. When the ball came to him and he let fire, his kick was wide, as it had been against South Africa in the World Cup, but this time the kick went to the right of the posts rather than the left and Wales were ahead rather than behind. Owens secured the drop-out with 80 seconds left and Wales, as they had done at Twickenham when down to 14 men, kept the ball among the forwards. France had to make a play for it, and when Attoub did so from an off-side position, Wales had a penalty on halfway. If they had kicked it, it would have maintained their record of winning every second half in the tournament, but time was up and Priestland kicked the ball high into the stand and the crowd started preparing to have a ball.

'The players have been a credit to Wales and they make the job of the coaches easy,' said Gatland in the after-match media conference. 'When you have them doing more than what we expect and what is required, and when you have them looking after themselves and doing all the extras, it goes a long way to making the coaches look good. We have accepted the tag of favourites, which has not always sat well on our shoulders. We have been down in games this year and we have learned to play ugly, which may not have been the case in the past. A young side has coped incredibly well and that can only be good for the next two to three years. Our big aim is to be consistent in beating the southern hemisphere teams and we are young enough to, I hope, be able to do that over the next few years.'

Saint-André felt Wales were lucky to win the grand slam. 'I don't think they will do it next year because they have to come to France and I hope, too, that the French clubs will buy all the fine Welsh players. If Wales had a red card for Bradley Davies against Ireland, I do not think they would finish the last 20 [*sic*] minutes with 14 men against 15 and win the game. Against England there were one or two crucial decisions and penalties can go one way or the other. It was also very close today.' He seemed to be speaking with the regret of a man who knew that an opportunity had passed him by. Were France lucky on the way to the grand slam in 2010 that Wales threw two passes against them in the first half in Cardiff that were more suicidal than risky?

It was not luck that Lydiate, who picked up his second man-of-the-match award of the tournament, was so often in the right place to make telling tackles. 'There has been a composure about us,' said Ryan Jones. 'We knew what we had to do and we knew we had the tools in our armoury to achieve it. We stuck to the job, weathering storms and shutting out the game. We are a team that plays for 80 minutes, as we showed against Ireland and England. You have to experience things to grow from them and this is still a relatively young squad.' Jones may not have been a regular starter, but his contribution from the start of the World Cup until the end of the Six Nations had been as telling as anyone's. The way he dealt with personal disappointment, at losing both the captaincy and then his place in the starting line-up, was not how it had always been with Wales down the years: the cause had too often been individual rather than common. It had become an accepted truth that Wales's revival was down to the younger members of the squad imposing their values on the seniors, but no better example was set than by Ryan Jones. What representing Wales meant to him was seen in two second-half incidents: when he beat Dusautoir to the ball after Harinordoquy's lineout steal and his sinew-straining tackle on a wing, Palisson.

The players who had appeared in all five matches could look forward to a cheque for some £90,000 in match fees, win bonuses and a lump sum for achieving the grand slam. They were also invited to the Senedd, the home of the Welsh Assembly government, for a reception on the Monday after the game. Wales capped 29 players during the tournament, 11 backs and 18 forwards. They were presented with Six Nations winners' medals after the victory over France, but Bradley Davies, who had been banned after the opening game in Dublin for foul play, was not at the Millennium Stadium. His medal turned up in the mail because he could not bring himself to go to the matches in Cardiff, but he was not there to sign for it and had to go to his local Post Office depot to retrieve it. 'I tried to stay local on the days when Wales were smashing everyone,' he said. 'I could have gone but my head was in the shed. I did not want to drag the boys down by lolling around. The medal has been waiting to get picked up. I stepped over the mark against Ireland and let my emotions get the better of me. I did not think it was too bad until I saw the incident on the big screen – it was terrible. I regret what I did but, most importantly, Donnacha Ryan was fine. I have to learn from this because I have lost my place in the Wales team and possibly my international future. All the second rows are playing well at the moment and my punishment could not have been worse. I lost out financially, but what cost me more was being the first-choice 4 for Wales and throwing it away.'

Lydiate was one player who never let his emotions corrupt his effectiveness. 'The path to paradise begins in hell,' wrote Dante in the Inferno section of his epic poem, *The Divine Comedy*. Lydiate had been on the excursion, with the scars to show for the experience, but as the Wales players went on their lap of honour and yet another rendition of 'Bread of Heaven' greeted the onset of evening, as far as one of their number went had ever such pain been turned into so much gain?

7

North and South

There were no illusions
On the summer side of life.

Gordon Lightfoot

Wales was not the only country where the 2012 grand slam was celebrated. The Australian Rugby Union thanked providence for giving them a means to market the three-Test series between the Wallabies and Wales that summer, a tour that included a midweek match against the Brumbies. It would be billed as a showdown between the champions of the two hemispheres, an unofficial world series between two countries who, more than any of their rivals, were prepared to cap players at a young age. Wales had the likes of George North, Alex Cuthbert, Leigh Halfpenny, Sam Warburton, Toby Faletau and Scott Williams, while Australia had James O'Connor, who like North had won his first cap at the age of 18, Kurtley Beale, Quade Cooper, David Pocock, Will Genia and Ben McCalman. The teams had met the previous October in the World Cup play-off, a repeat of 1987; on both occasions, the game was won by the team less grief-stricken at not reaching the final. Australia were well beaten by the eventual winners New Zealand in 2011 a day after Wales went down to France by a point, having missed potentially match-winning kicks. Australia's 21–18 victory to take the bronze medal was more convincing than the scoreboard suggested, as was their 24–18 success in Cardiff six weeks later when Shane Williams marked the end of his international career by scoring his 58th try for Wales with his last touch of the ball.

Wales had not beaten Australia since 2008, the year of their previous grand slam, and their one failing under Gatland had been against the might of the southern hemisphere. Wales's success rate in the Six Nations under Gatland was 72 per cent: in the 1960s it was (in the old Five Nations) 55 per cent, nearly 80 per cent in the 1970s, 46 per cent in the 1980s, 31 per cent in the 1990s and in the 2000s, before Gatland's arrival, it was 40 per cent. What had remained a constant was failure against New Zealand, South Africa and, after the 1970s, Australia. After losing to Wales in 1953, the All Blacks won in 1963, 1967, 1969 (twice), 1972, 1978, 1980, 1987, 1988 (twice), 1989, 1995, 1997, 2002, 2003 (twice), 2004, 2005, 2006, 2008, 2009 and 2010. Wales's first and, at the time of writing, only victory against South Africa came in 1999. Their post-war record against the Springboks saw defeats in 1951, 1960, 1964, 1994, 1995, 1996, two in 1998, 1999, 2000, two in 2002, two in 2004, 2005, 2007, three in 2008, two in 2010 and 2011 interrupted by a draw in 1970. The record against the Wallabies, whose best period came from the end of the 1970s, was better. Wales won eight and lost five between 1908 and 1987, but in nineteen Tests after that they had won two, in 2005 and 2008, and lost sixteen, drawing in 2006. Their one victory on Australian soil had come in Sydney in 1969, when Gerald Davies scored his first try after being converted from a centre to a wing.

'There is no doubt that Wales's triumph in the Six

197

Nations has been recognised in Australia,' said the ARU's chief executive John O'Neill at the end of March. 'What was already considerable interest in the tour has been heightened and of all the European teams we could have had coming to us this year, Wales are unquestionably the pick. They not only have an impressive team, full of young and talented players, but they play an attractive style of rugby. Another factor is the Lions tour here in 2013. The word is that Warren Gatland will be the head coach and his presence with Wales, up against our head coach Robbie Deans, will give the series an added piquancy. It is the first time we have played three internationals against one country in the same month for a number of years and we will have sell-outs in Brisbane and Sydney for sure and, we expect, Melbourne. The venues are in the same sequence as they will be for the Lions and the final game will be played at the Sydney Football Stadium, which last staged an international back in 1998, and it has a 3 p.m. kick-off. The return to an afternoon Test has been very popular and rugby followers here are expecting a hard-fought series. We do have a good recent record against Wales, but they have made significant strides under Gatland and we are well aware that he sees the next stage in his side's development in terms of securing victories against the major southern hemisphere nations. We will be looking to gain momentum ahead of our new Rugby Championship, which will be fought for by the old Tri-Nations teams and Argentina, as well as put down a marker ahead of the Lions tour. Wales showed in the World Cup that they are one of the leading teams in the world and they look as if they are still far from being at their peak.'

Gatland was interviewed by the Lions committee five days after Wales won the grand slam, before he returned to New Zealand for a holiday. The other candidates were the Ireland head coach Declan Kidney and Scotland's Andy Robinson. Gatland was offered the position, subject to the Welsh Rugby Union agreeing to release him from his contract. The Lions had long stated that they wanted the head coach for the Australia tour to be available to them on an exclusive basis for 12 months before the trip. That meant Gatland would not have been able to take Wales to Australia, nor be in charge for the November international programme that contained Tests against Argentina, Samoa, New Zealand and Australia. The WRU was willing to free Gatland from the 2013 Six Nations campaign, accepting that he would need to then be free to visit the other home unions, speaking to players and coaches and taking in matches, but it insisted Gatland would be on the 2012 summer tour Down Under and it wanted him to prepare the side against New Zealand and Australia the following autumn. Formal talks between the WRU and the Lions did not start until the first week of April with Gatland having admitted interest in the position. 'I know I am in the frame and the Union has given me support for that,' he said a few hours after the victory over France. 'It would be a huge honour if the offer came along, but there are a number of things to be put in place before that and we do not know what their requirements are.'

There were two other concerns for the WRU to confront as it reflected on its best international season since the 1970s: when Wales reached the semi-final of the World Cup in 1987, they won their first three matches in the Five Nations, clinching the triple crown in Dublin. They had to beat France in Cardiff to secure the grand slam, but lost by a point in the rain – some of the spectators in the old National Stadium were not protected by a roof in those days, never mind the entire ground. Clubs in France, backed by multi-millionaires, were now casting a covetous gaze towards Wales at a time when the four regions were in such financial straits that they collectively agreed to observe a £3.5m salary cap for the 2012–13 season. The WRU had at the end of January commissioned the global professional services firm PricewaterhouseCoopers to examine the finances of the regions, and the Union itself. It was due to submit its report within three months and, as the Top 14 clubs circled, Cardiff Blues, Newport Gwent Dragons, the Scarlets and Ospreys asked some players, like Cuthbert, to delay contract negotiations until they knew what the future would look like: the fear was that the number would either be cut to three or that the WRU would reduce the money received by one of the regions from central funds, making it more of a development side. Peter Thomas, the chairman of the Blues, had warned at the start of the Six Nations that the regions would no longer pay their international players when they were away with Wales, which amounted to more than one-third of a year. 'Rugby is our national sport, but sadly it is not reflected in regional rugby and that's backed up by the fact that we're not getting the crowds that we used to have, and desperately need,' said Thomas. 'It is a great worry and the regions have had to introduce a salary cap. If you look at a national squad player, he is available to his region for only 20 weeks a year. In any business you cannot afford to pay someone with the crowds that we're getting, or the lack of them, and the way the game is going it cannot be sustained any longer by private equity. It's unsustainable as it is and we are looking at various modules, working very closely with the Welsh Rugby Union. I'm very optimistic that the four regions can survive as sustainable businesses on the basis of discipline and working within lower, tighter, stricter budgets. The time has come when we've now got to work within our means. Effectively you've got to take more money in than what you spend out and to do that there has to be cuts.'

The WRU wanted to introduce central contracts when regional rugby was established in 2003, but received no support from the regions. Its reaction to the problems facing the four in 2012 was to call for a sea change in attitude. 'We are at a fundamental crossroads in the history of Welsh rugby,' said the Union's chief executive, Roger Lewis, on BBC Radio Wales. 'We are at a critical stage and that's what is so exciting because if we get this right we will come up with something in world rugby that will be the envy of it. We've got to think differently. We cannot think we've just got to fix what's gone on before. We've got to come up with something that's far more radical and far more sustainable, that will take our game forward.' Central contracts would be one strand.

As soon as the Wales players left the Vale of Glamorgan the day after winning the grand slam, they were back on duty with their regions. Gatland wanted those who had played a full part in the campaign to be given the week off, but he could only make a request to the regional directors of rugby, not insist. The former Wales full-back J.P.R. Williams made a call in the week after the grand slam for the regional system to be dismantled and replaced by an eight-club league. He described regional rugby as dire and disgraceful and asked why players who stood out in international rugby looked so poor when they returned to their regions.

His remarks were made on a day when Regional Rugby Wales, the umbrella organisation of the four professional sides, held a media conference at Cardiff City Stadium to celebrate the achievement of the Wales squad. All the Wales-based players who had taken part in the Six Nations turned out in their regional kit ahead of that weekend's local derbies. It was essentially a photo-opportunity, but Williams's remarks, as well as the impending report from the review, gave it an edge. 'Wales have won three grand slams in the regional era,' said RRW's chief executive, Stuart Gallacher. 'They did not manage one in the last 25 years of the club system. J.P.R. Williams's comments stagger me, and how is it that a person of his acumen could come out with a statement so full of nonsense? It is only a short time ago that we had nine clubs, did not win anything and were beaten in Europe by sixty points. Where will the money and players come for eight teams? It beggars belief, but he is not connected to the professional game and his opinion does not hold water. The regions and I are disappointed. We have to remember we are in the middle of one of the biggest recessions this country has ever seen. One of the first things to go is not an international ticket but one for a regional game. Everyone is working hard in the regions, but international rugby is an event. We need three things, starting with sustainability – we cannot have the same problems next year. Second, it is vital we keep our best players in Wales and I think we can: we have not lost a lot, but we have lost some, which is too many. We used to lose players to rugby league, now it is to France, where clubs have a lot of money. And then, third, we can push forward to be competitive again. The current Welsh squad is competitive and we are expanding the base of players. I hope there is a spin-off from the grand slam for the regions. It is an important back-end of the season for us. We need to understand what we can afford and achieve at regional level. A recession like this crystallises minds. I have enormous respect for the people who have invested their money in clubs and regions in Wales and kept players in the country, but there comes a time when that kind of input is no longer viable and we have reached it. The financial review will be considered by a steering group made up of representatives from the WRU and regions. We need to get the right numbers and information so we can act accordingly but I see going from four regions to three as a step back, not forward. I am optimistic because it is our national game. It just needs a huge effort from everyone.'

As Gallacher was speaking, reports were circulating in France that Toulouse were interested in signing Dan Lydiate and Toulon were checking up on Alex Cuthbert. 'I have another season with the Dragons,' said Lydiate. 'I do not like to look too far ahead, not really beyond the next game because you can always pick up bumps. It would be nice to go to Australia in the summer, but there is a lot of rugby to be played between now and then. I want to have a good campaign with the Dragons next season and I want to stay in Wales and play for Wales, which means doing well for your region. A few boys are leaving now and you want your best players to be in Wales. Our success has made Welsh players known on the global stage, starting with the World Cup, and it is a double-edged sword.' Cuthbert was negotiating his first professional contract with the Blues but had been told to wait. 'A lot of the boys are leaving but my aim is to stay in Wales and I want to play for the Blues,' he told the *South Wales Echo*. 'If things don't work out, I will need to have other options. My agent has looked outside the box, which you can't blame me or him for doing. We are in negotiations with French clubs, but we're just talking about things at the moment. It is about seeing what else is on offer. I am hoping the Blues can offer me something I can be comfortable with and provide a competitive offer for me to sign. They have asked me to wait another week or two and I am trusting them to get this sorted.'

Matthew Rees was one of the few players in the Wales squad whose career straddled the club and regional eras. He played for Pontypridd in the Welsh Premiership before spending his first year in the regional game with Celtic

Warriors, who were disbanded by the WRU after one season, and then joining the Scarlets. 'The regional system has made our rugby a lot more professional and we are getting stronger and stronger,' he said. 'We have closed the gap on the best teams in the world in terms of professionalism and the players coming through the system now know exactly what it takes to be a rugby player at the highest level. We are in a good position on the international front and we need to keep working hard at regional level. There is a lot of talent out there and it is important we keep improving season by season. A significant difference now is that when we lose a player of influence, like Shane Williams, Alex Cuthbert comes in and steps up to the mark straight away.'

Rees was concerned at the impact the free-spending French could have on the regions. 'It is vital that we keep the best players in Wales and we have to target the regional game,' he said. 'We play before sell-out crowds at the Millennium Stadium, but the attendances in the regions have not been as high as we would like. I think there are a number of factors, such as the timing of kick-offs and Thursday night rugby. It is something that needs to be looked at. Overall, we have to be pleased with the way the game is going and we have to build on it. Youngsters coming through in Wales need to see the likes of Jamie Roberts and George North still playing here. We have lost Gethin Jenkins, Mike Phillips, James Hook and Huw Bennett. It is a worry to me as a player and it is something we need to correct. If the regions are to be successful, challenging in the RaboDirect Pro 12 and Heineken Cup, they need to be able to keep hold of their top players. We have had a big Six Nations and I hope that has a knock-on effect. If players go abroad, they are not available for all the national training camps and there is disruption during the Six Nations when they have to return to their clubs. I think Ireland have it right with central contracts, which allow them to look after their players. They tend to only play in the big games for their provinces and they come into international periods fresh. Player welfare is an issue, how many games you play in a season may have an effect on your career and how long it lasts and there is the issue of recovery time. Central contracts would be a step in the right direction for us. It would mean international players were looked after. At the moment, when you finish a tournament like the Six Nations you go straight back to your region and, understandably, they want you to play right away. Central contracts would mean the Wales coach could give his players time off when he felt they needed it. That will be the next step for the professional game here. We face a big end to the campaign for the regions, three Tests in Australia, next season and then the Lions tour. It is non-stop and that is where central contracts could play a big part for the players.'

Rees made his debut for Wales after the 2005 grand slam. He had played under four coaches at international level and felt that under Gatland they had established themselves as a major force again. 'One thing Warren Gatland has brought in is that we work harder than anyone else and we have a mental toughness now,' he said. 'It is part of our training environment and the players do not shirk away from anything. In the past, we would stay with southern hemisphere teams for 50 or 60 minutes and then fold, but now we have the fitness to stay with them. Poland changed attitudes. I had never trained so hard in my life. We were taken to the limit and it gave us the confidence to go to the next level. There was no doubt in my mind in the build-up to the France game: there was going to be one winner and that was us. The challenge in the Six Nations was to build on what had been achieved in the World Cup. We had three home games and were tagged as one of the favourites, but our first game was away to Ireland when we had a number of forwards injured. It was always going to be a tough ask, but what we showed that day was that we had developed considerable strength in depth and that we had a frightening back line. Everyone knows they have to be playing well week in, week out because there is a youngster knocking at the door. The next level for us is to beat a southern hemisphere team. We put up a big fight in the World Cup against South Africa and were unlucky against Australia. The confidence and the belief are there. We know we have a lot to work on individually and collectively. The pressure was on us against France and we have not had that tag in the past. We have shown we can handle it.'

As Roger Lewis waited to receive the results of the PricewaterhouseCoopers review, he reflected on a period of unprecedented growth for the WRU. 'Not everything in the garden is rosy, and we are going to front up to that, but the Union is in its best state in its 131-year history,' he said. 'We have decreased our debt by £20m in the last five years and we will be debt-free by 2021. We have achieved growth of 13.4 per cent in the last five years and we will again post record financial results. We are able to invest in the game more than ever before. We have built a national centre for excellence, we run the five regional academies, which includes one in the north of Wales, and we have established a pathway for young players that I would say is the best around. I see what is happening with the regions as a huge opportunity for the game in Wales. We are working with everyone concerned and it is a matter of applying joined-up thinking, creating a new model that is based on the best interests of Welsh rugby.

'At international level, our faith in Warren Gatland has been amply repaid and we have contracted all of his management team to at least the 2015 World Cup. We have all of the right people in all of the right places. I talk to Warren on a regular basis and you have to respect what he has done for Wales. He will have been here for eight years by the time of the next World Cup, a considerable commitment. What he does after that I do not know: his first commitment has to be his family. He is someone who is very comfortable in his own skin and he will make the decisions that are right for him. The Australia series is important for us and we will be taking our largest-ever squad abroad in what is our most exciting tour in years. You have to have ambition and a desire to make a mark on the world. I think the group of players we have in the senior squad, together with the young ones coming through the system, serve as a metaphor for modern Wales with their creativity, youthfulness, hard work, ambition and dedication. We have the right environment and the right culture.'

Wales had won grand slams in clusters, three between 1908 and 1911, two in the early 1950s, three in the 1970s and three from 2005. They went thirty-nine years without one from 1911, nineteen years from 1952 and twenty-seven years from 1978. History suggested a fallow period awaited, at least in terms of grand slams, but Gatland's Wales looked capable of breaking the mould. They started the year eighth in the world rankings; after defeating England they moved up to fourth, the position where they needed to be at the end of the year to avoid finding themselves in a pool with the holders New Zealand or Australia or South Africa in the 2015 World Cup. England's victory over France in Paris took them above Wales and they finished the Six Nation ranked fourth, behind New Zealand, Australia and South Africa. Wales had eight matches left in 2012: the Barbarians at the Millennium Stadium in June, three Tests in Australia and an autumn series in Cardiff against Argentina, Samoa, the All Blacks and the Wallabies. Gatland's policy has been to expose his players to the leading southern hemisphere nations every year. The first six fixtures between Wales and Australia were spread out over sixty-one years; the next six covered eighteen years. By December 2012, Wales would have played Australia six times in thirteen months. From the moment he arrived in Wales at the end of 2007, Gatland was resolute in his belief that to become the best, you had to take on the best, not hide away. In the professional era, Wales had played the three major southern hemisphere nations forty-six times up to the end of 2011, winning three, drawing one and losing the rest. They had been getting increasingly close under Gatland, especially against South Africa, but his one victory had been against the 2008 Wallabies.

Dean Malone, writing on the Australian sports website The Roar at the end of March 2012, seemed to sum up the attitude in the south to the north when he wrote: 'With the Six Nations over, attention in the northern hemisphere is now on the upcoming mid-year internationals. Expectations up north are, as always, quite high. But realistically, what are England [who were going to South Africa in the summer], Ireland [who had a series in New Zealand] and Wales's chances of heading across the equator and scoring a few upsets? Very little I suspect. The last time Australia lost against Wales was on 29 November 2008, in Wales. The Welsh have tasted victory on Australian soil only once, way back in 1969. Australia's all-time winning percentage at home is 59.45, but that figure since 2000 increases to 78.16. Wales under Warren Gatland have been known to talk a bit too much and that is fine. But they have to back it up against the best opposition. Wales are undoubtedly a good team, but they lack the composure and self-belief to turn over the Big

Three. Australia have the players to win this one. People may say the stats count for nothing, but I think it paints an accurate picture of what will happen come the June tests. Despite South Africa losing many old hands, they have a new coach, and many new faces coming through with better talent than what is on offer in England. Even England have two [*sic*] South Africans in their side. Australia have some stability with new players putting up their hands on a weekly basis. And the All Blacks: well, when have we ever seen a poor All Blacks team? All this leads to the continued dominance of world rugby by the southern hemisphere.'

Lydiate acknowledged the size of the task facing Wales. 'I do not see why we cannot win the series in Australia,' he said. 'It will be some challenge because we will be taken out of our comfort zone of the Millennium Stadium, but the boys are looking forward to it and it should be interesting. We are confident in our ability as a squad, but we do not let that get to us. We concentrate on the next training session and the next game and if you do that you cannot go too far wrong.' North was another player who was not weighed down by the past: what mattered to him was not how Wales had performed against the might of the south in the past, but how they compared with them in the present. It reflected the mood of the new Wales: *carpe diem* – seize the moment. 'We have beaten the teams in the northern hemisphere so now the next big thing is the southern hemisphere,' said North. 'That is where the best teams in the world are – Australia, South Africa and New Zealand. Our next step as a country has to be to cement the fact we are one of the best teams in the world and that means going to Australia and beating them on their own turf. I think this squad is ready to do that. We are a young team with some older heads and I think we have the right characters. We have great strength in depth now and everyone is fighting for their place in the team. The standard has been pushed up and that is going to make us stronger going into the summer.'

Rugby in Wales in the 1970s was seen as poetry, but the professional era was prose. At the end of December 2011, the Welsh novelist, poet and playwright Owen Sheers was appointed the WRU's first writer-in-residence in a three-year initiative funded by the Welsh Arts Council: two other artists would take over in the succeeding years. Sheers's brief was to examine the drama and cultural impact of the country's national game and he would be given access behind the scenes. 'I have a privileged opportunity not just to examine events on the field, but to look at supporters, fitness coaches, families, the whole thing,' he said. 'I'm going in with an open mind. It's one of the reasons why I accepted the position, because some writers-in-residence are asked to write something immediately, which sometimes leads to poor work. I can't say what form it will take. It could be a book of fiction, it could be a book of short stories, a play or a poem.'

Sheers was given a page in each of the three match programmes in the 2012 Six Nations. His first contribution, on the day of the Scotland match, was a poem entitled 'Song at the Year's Turning' and it contained the lines:

> We are grown from memory but are alive only now,
>   our past breaths upon the wind.
> So whatever has been done, through there, is gone;
>   whoever sinned,
> whoever won is recalled and forgotten here, in this
>   place where the glory, bruise and blame
> will all be washed away by now. The new grass shall
>   purge us in its flame.

The present was purging the past. The 1970s had become

a fading signpost to glory, a breath upon the wind, but the path was now leading elsewhere. 'I am convinced this can be another golden era for Wales,' said Gallacher, who was capped by Wales against France as a second row in 1970 before turning professional with Bradford Northern. 'It must be the biggest team we have ever fielded. The players are massive but they are so comfortable on the big stage. They are relaxed in their own ability and they are a credit to Wales, the regions and the 300 clubs in the country who produce players.'

Wales had in the 1970s been underpinned by a club system that, so the legend at the time went, was the envy of the rugby world. There is a danger in romanticising the past, but 19 so-called first-class clubs, operating long before a league system was introduced, generated considerable interest, supported by the grassroots below them. Derbies were played every week and players, with a few exceptions like Mervyn Davies, had to prove themselves at club level before being chosen to play in the trial between the Probables and the Possibles that was held before the start of the Five Nations. The leading players were known by their first names or initials at the start of the decade, Barry, Gareth, Gerald, Merv, J.P.R., Delme, J.J., and by the end they were Benny, Gravs, Pricey, Cobs, a familiarity that reflected an identity with the Welsh public. After the 2012 Six Nations, Lydiate smiled when asked if he was recognised everywhere he went in Wales. His scrum-cap, he said, gave him an invisibility that allowed him to walk largely undetected; when Barry John retired at the age of twenty-seven in 1972, one year after the Lions won the series against the All Blacks, he said he had become a celebrity rather than a rugby player and feared it would undermine his performances on the field. He was the game's first superstar, but he only wanted to be noticed on a rugby field.

The Welsh Grand Slam 2012

'It has been a real pleasure to watch this side grow in stature over the past couple of months and they fully deserve to be called Europe's finest,' wrote John in his column in *Wales on Sunday* at the end of the 2012 Six Nations. 'The next challenge, three Tests in Australia, will be a lot harder. But Wales will be competitive, their wonderful defence will see to that, and we hope they can take the next step. Graham Henry, when he was in charge of Wales, used to talk about how inexperience in the closing ten minutes of matches proved so costly during his tenure. He was making the point that Wales just didn't have the knack or know-how of closing out tight games. This team under Gatland is younger than Henry's side, but they already clearly have that very thing that was missing in yesteryear.'

Gatland, a hard, pragmatic New Zealander, was under no illusions about what lay ahead. In 2010, he had been criticised in the Welsh media for being a conservative coach, someone who enchained his players rather than empowered them; there were matches in which Wales seemed to fall back on Shane Williams's brilliance, but Gatland had always been about players operating with their heads up and reacting to what was in front of them; it just took him a while to convince his charges he meant what he said. Before the fixture against Scotland in 2012, he talked about the review of the Ireland game the previous weekend that he had just held with his players. 'One of their tries came indirectly from a lineout,' he said. 'We had kicked the ball into touch from near our own line, but at the time there were two players free on the outside. My message was that it did not matter where you were on the field, if there was a move on, go for it. It is all about appreciating the right moment and it never has been the case that you should only move the ball in certain areas of the field.'

There were numerous right moments in 2012: Priestland's deftness in creating Jonathan Davies's first try in Dublin; North's rampage and back-of-the-hand pass for Davies's second; Halfpenny's strength of mind to kick the winning penalty and the courage the full-back displayed throughout the tournament, encapsulated in the challenge he made on David Strettle in the final play of the game at Twickenham to deny England the chance to draw level; Ryan Jones coming on as a replacement against France and making a telling contribution immediately; Scott Williams's moment of inspiration at Twickenham, reminiscent of the impact Ray 'Chico' Hopkins had made at the same ground 42 years before after replacing Gareth Edwards; Alex Cuthbert's winning try against France when he appreciated his speed rather than size was what was required; Gethin Jenkins imposing himself at the breakdown, a prop with the mind of a flanker; Adam Jones, a player who in 2004 had tended to be taken off after 30 minutes because he was not deemed fit enough, hitting rucks at the end of the matches with the same force as at the beginning; Toby Faletau, a man of almost no words off the pitch who did his shouting on it; Ian Evans, the resurrection man who made a perceived weakness of Wales's at the beginning of the tournament into a strength; Alun Wyn Jones's ability to force vital turnovers; Sam Warburton's tackle on Manu Tuilagi and his composure in the heat of battle; Matthew Rees turning disappointment into triumph; the way Mike Phillips held Wales together after Priestland's yellow card against England; Jamie Roberts's try against Italy, like Cuthbert seeing that space, not contact, held the key; and Dan Lydiate, an unassuming man whose tackles were as hard as his voice was soft.

Asked what his abiding memory of 2012 would be, Lydiate replied: 'Walking round Twickenham with the triple crown was awesome. It was the first bit of silverware

I had ever won and it will live long in my memory.' He had been given the week off by the Dragons, but was not going to revel in the grand slam. 'I will go back to Llandrindod Wells this weekend and see everyone. It clears my head. I do miss living at the farm and helping out. I hope to settle down there after my career is over.'

The last word deserves to go to Warburton. 'We do not talk about what we could accomplish,' he said. 'People make comparisons with the 1970s and the legends who played in that time but you just crack on because you do not perceive yourself in the same way. No one has spoken any further than the next game, so you do not have to try to keep feet on the ground. It seems everyone is already speaking about 2015: we are aware that it is being held in England but it has never been mentioned in the squad. No one has a clue about what will happen then, but what is exciting is that this group could potentially be together for years to come. We get on very well and are doing OK at the moment. I am not religious or superstitious, but after we had lost the World Cup semi-final to France, I had one of the stupid feelings I get every now and then. I thought something good would happen and we thoroughly deserved the grand slam. We had worked hard and made sacrifices. The semi-final disappointment spurred us on and made us stronger. Now we have to get a scalp in the southern hemisphere.'

Statistics

AVIVA STADIUM - 05.02.12

15	Kearney	1	Healy
14	Bowe	2	Best
13	McFadden	3	Ross
12	D'Arcy	4	O'Callaghan
11	Trimble	5	**O'Connell**
10	Sexton	6	Ferris
9	Murray	7	O'Brien
		8	Heaslip

IRELAND 21   **WALES 23**

10	HT	5

15	Halfpenny	1	Gill
14	Cuthbert	2	Bennett
13	J J V Davies	3	A R Jones
12	Roberts	4	B S Davies
11	North	5	Evans
10	Priestland	6	R P Jones
9	Phillips	7	**Warburton**
		8	Faletau

GRAHAM TIMING

		IRELAND			
Try	**2**	PenTry	0		
Conversions	1 / 2				
Penalty Goals	3 / 5				
Drop Goals	0 / 1				

Phases of Play

Scrums Won	2
Lost	0
Lineouts Won	5
Lost	0
Pens Conceded	6
Freekick Conceded	1
Mauls Won	1
Ruck and Drive	21
Ruck and Pass	58

Ball Won

In Open Play	80
In Opponent's 22	16
At Set Pieces	14
Turnovers Won	4

Team Statistics

Passes Completed	153
Line Breaks	2
Possession Kicked	30
Errors from Kicks	2
Kicks to Touch	9
Percentage Kicks	61%
Tackles Made	127
Missed	9
Tackle Completion	93%
Offloads in Tackle	6
Offloads / Tackled	6%
Total Errors Made	8
Errors / Possession	16%

Minutes in Possession

1	18:18	2	14:07

Mins in Opponent's Half

1	18:19	2	17:32

Match timeline

SEXTON - Penalty	03:37	
	13:53	J J V DAVIES - Try
	14:26	PRIESTLAND - ConMiss
	18:50	PRIESTLAND - PenMiss
SEXTON - DropMiss	27:13	
SEXTON - PenMiss	28:04	
BEST - Try	36:51	
SEXTON - Conversion	38:30	
	HT	
	40:03	Tipuric on for Warburton
	40:05	Hook on for Cuthbert
SEXTON - Penalty	43:08	
	49:10	PRIESTLAND - PenMiss
	53:15	HALFPENNY - Penalty
	54:42	J J V DAVIES - Try
	55:45	HALFPENNY - Conversion
SEXTON - Penalty	59:51	
Ryan on for O'callaghan	62:53	
	64:53	B S DAVIES - Sin Bin
	67:58	J J V DAVIES - Try
SEXTON - ConMiss	69:41	
	69:49	James on for A R Jones
SEXTON - PenMiss	73:44	
Court on for Healy	73:55	
	75:55	NORTH - Try
	76:38	HALFPENNY - ConMiss
O'gara on for Sexton	76:47	
Reddan on for Murray	76:49	
FERRIS - Sin Bin	79:06	
	79:33	HALFPENNY - Penalty

		WALES			
Try	**3**	PenTry	0		
Conversions	1 / 3				
Penalty Goals	2 / 4				
Drop Goals	0 / 0				

Phases of Play

Scrums Won	3
Lost	0
Lineouts Won	10
Lost	4
Pens Conceded	7
Freekick Conceded	1
Mauls Won	1
Ruck and Drive	22
Ruck and Pass	90

Ball Won

In Open Play	113
In Opponent's 22	17
At Set Pieces	19
Turnovers Won	2

Team Statistics

Passes Completed	201
Line Breaks	2
Possession Kicked	22
Errors from Kicks	1
Kicks to Touch	5
Percentage Kicks	45%
Tackles Made	94
Missed	9
Tackle Completion	91%
Offloads in Tackle	3
Offloads / Tackled	2%
Total Errors Made	4
Errors / Possession	8%

Minutes in Possession

1	21:42	2	18:12

Mins in Opponent's Half

1	27:23	2	27:57

Match Facts are recorded under the guidance and direction of KEN HARROWER (SRRA/SRU REFEREE)

05.02.12		17:02

MILLENNIUM STADIUM - 12.02.12

15	Halfpenny	1	Jenkins
14	Cuthbert	2	Bennett
13	J J Davies	3	A R Jones
12	Roberts	4	**R P Jones**
11	North	5	Evans
10	Priestland	6	Lydiate
9	Phillips	7	Shingler
		8	Faletau

WALES	SCOTLAND
27	**13**

3	HT	3

15	R P Lamont	1	Jacobsen
14	Jones	2	**Ford**
13	de Luca	3	Cross
12	S F Lamont	4	Gray
11	Evans	5	Hamilton
10	Laidlaw	6	Strokosch
9	Cusiter	7	Rennie
		8	Denton

GRAHAM TIMING

WALES

Try	3	PenTry	0
Conversions		3 / 3	
Penalty Goals		2 / 3	
Drop Goals		0 / 0	

Phases of Play

Scrums Won	3
Lost	0
Lineouts Won	10
Lost	2
Pens Conceded	13
Freekick Conceded	2
Mauls Won	1
Ruck and Drive	8
Ruck and Pass	60

Ball Won

In Open Play	69
In Opponent's 22	34
At Set Pieces	22
Turnovers Won	3

Team Statistics

Passes Completed	154
Line Breaks	7
Possession Kicked	26
Errors from Kicks	1
Kicks to Touch	2
Percentage Kicks	39%
Tackles Made	178
Missed	16
Tackle Completion	91%
Offloads in Tackle	10
Offloads / Tackled	10%
Total Errors Made	10
Errors / Possession	15%

Minutes in Possession

1	10:53	2	17:07

Mins in Opponent's Half

1	20:43	2	25:26

Centre timeline

Wales	Time	Scotland
	05:26	LAIDLAW - PenMiss
Owens on for Bennett	09:44	
	15:37	Hogg on for Evans
Bennett on for Owens	18:49	
	22:40	LAIDLAW - Penalty
HALFPENNY - Penalty	29:41	
Hook on for North	39:36	
	HT	
Owens on for Bennett	40:00	
CUTHBERT - Try	41:50	
	42:59	Barclay on for Strokosch
HALFPENNY - Conversion	43:11	
	44:52	DE LUCA - Sin Bin
HALFPENNY - Penalty	45:56	
	48:04	LAIDLAW - Penalty
	48:04	Blair on for Cusiter
HALFPENNY - Try	50:49	
HALFPENNY - Conversion	52:03	
	53:07	R P LAMONT - Sin Bin
HALFPENNY - Try	55:29	
	56:50	Kalman on for Cross
HALFPENNY - Conversion	56:51	
	57:14	Kellock on for Hamilton
	63:49	LAIDLAW - Try
	64:43	LAIDLAW - Conversion
HALFPENNY - PenMiss	68:54	
	71:03	S Lawson on for Ford
Powell on for Lydiate	72:22	
James on for A R Jones	72:22	
L D Williams on for Phillips	73:08	
Reed on for R P Jones	74:28	
JENKINS - Sin Bin	77:03	
M S Williams on for Roberts	77:19	

SCOTLAND

Try	1	PenTry	0
Conversions		1 / 1	
Penalty Goals		2 / 3	
Drop Goals		0 / 0	

Phases of Play

Scrums Won	3
Lost	0
Lineouts Won	7
Lost	0
Pens Conceded	9
Freekick Conceded	1
Mauls Won	2
Ruck and Drive	27
Ruck and Pass	111

Ball Won

In Open Play	140
In Opponent's 22	35
At Set Pieces	23
Turnovers Won	1

Team Statistics

Passes Completed	254
Line Breaks	5
Possession Kicked	19
Errors from Kicks	0
Kicks to Touch	3
Percentage Kicks	29%
Tackles Made	99
Missed	9
Tackle Completion	91%
Offloads in Tackle	19
Offloads / Tackled	10%
Total Errors Made	8
Errors / Possession	12%

Minutes in Possession

1	17:32	2	17:43

Mins in Opponent's Half

1	20:41	2	18:37

Match Facts are recorded under the guidance and direction of KEN HARROWER (SRRA/SRU REFEREE)

12.02.12		17:02

TWICKENHAM - 25.02.12

15	Foden	1	Corbisiero
14	Ashton	2	Hartley
13	Tuilagi	3	Cole
12	Barritt	4	Botha
11	Strettle	5	Parling
10	Farrell	6	Croft
9	Dickson	7	**Robshaw**
		8	Morgan

15	Halfpenny	1	Jenkins
14	Cuthbert	2	Owens
13	J J V Davies	3	A R Jones
12	Roberts	4	A W Jones
11	North	5	Evans
10	Priestland	6	Lydiate
9	Phillips	7	**Warburton**
		8	Faletau

ENGLAND 12 **WALES 19**

9	HT	6

GRAHAM TIMING

	ENGLAND			Time		WALES	
Try	**0**	PenTry	0				
Conversions		**0 / 0**		19:16	HALFPENNY - PenMiss		
Penalty Goals		**4 / 5**		22:32	FARRELL - DropMiss		
Drop Goals		**0 / 1**		23:44	FARRELL - Penalty		
				25:56	HALFPENNY - Penalty		
Phases of Play				29:06	FARRELL - Penalty		
Scrums Won		1		34:16	HALFPENNY - Penalty		
Lost		0		38:42	FARRELL - Penalty		
Lineouts Won		8		HT			
Lost		1		40:26	M S Williams on for Roberts		
Pens Conceded		13		44:28	PRIESTLAND - Sin Bin		
Freekick Conceded		1		45:13	FARRELL - Penalty		
Mauls Won		3		53:44	HALFPENNY - Penalty		
Ruck and Drive		21		53:57	R P Jones on for A W Jones		
Ruck and Pass		60		60:50	Lawes on for Botha		
				60:50	Youngs on for Dickson		
Ball Won				63:44	FARRELL - PenMiss		
In Open Play		84		65:53	Flood on for Farrell		
In Opponent's 22		8		65:53	Stevens on for Corbisiero		
At Set Pieces		21		71:39	HALFPENNY - Penalty		
Turnovers Won		5		72:11	Dowson on for Morgan		
				72:13	Webber on for Hartley		
Team Statistics				75:20	M S WILLIAMS - Try		
Passes Completed		163		76:06	HALFPENNY - Conversion		
Line Breaks		1		77:44	Brown on for Foden		

ENGLAND

Try	**0**	PenTry	0
Conversions	**0 / 0**
Penalty Goals	**4 / 5**
Drop Goals	**0 / 1**

Phases of Play

Scrums Won	1
Lost	0
Lineouts Won	8
Lost	1
Pens Conceded	13
Freekick Conceded	1
Mauls Won	3
Ruck and Drive	21
Ruck and Pass	60

Ball Won

In Open Play	84
In Opponent's 22	8
At Set Pieces	21
Turnovers Won	5

Team Statistics

Passes Completed	163
Line Breaks	1
Possession Kicked	23
Errors from Kicks	5
Kicks to Touch	5
Percentage Kicks	41%
Tackles Made	110
Missed	12
Tackle Completion	90%
Offloads in Tackle	6
Offloads / Tackled	6%
Total Errors Made	14
Errors / Possession	25%

Minutes in Possession

1	12:09	2	**14:35**

Mins in Opponent's Half

1	19:52	2	**24:01**

WALES

Try	**1**	PenTry	0
Conversions	**1 / 1**
Penalty Goals	**4 / 5**
Drop Goals	**0 / 0**

Phases of Play

Scrums Won	2
Lost	0
Lineouts Won	9
Lost	2
Pens Conceded	12
Freekick Conceded	1
Mauls Won	2
Ruck and Drive	48
Ruck and Pass	42

Ball Won

In Open Play	92
In Opponent's 22	6
At Set Pieces	24
Turnovers Won	5

Team Statistics

Passes Completed	134
Line Breaks	3
Possession Kicked	22
Errors from Kicks	5
Kicks to Touch	1
Percentage Kicks	40%
Tackles Made	99
Missed	9
Tackle Completion	91%
Offloads in Tackle	7
Offloads / Tackled	6%
Total Errors Made	9
Errors / Possession	16%

Minutes in Possession

1	**13:24**	2	14:04

Mins in Opponent's Half

1	**21:17**	2	18:45

Match Facts are recorded under the guidance and direction of STEPHEN P SMITH (WRU REFEREE)

25.02.12		18:25

MILLENNIUM STADIUM - 10.03.12

15	Halfpenny	1	**Jenkins**
14	Cuthbert	2	Rees
13	J J V Davies	3	A R Jones
12	Roberts	4	A W Jones
11	North	5	Evans
10	Priestland	6	Lydiate
9	Phillips	7	Tipuric
		8	Faletau

WALES 24 — ITALY 3

9 | HT | 3

15	Masi	1	Lo Cicero
14	MI Bergamasco	2	Ghiraldini
13	Canale	3	Cittadini
12	Sgarbi	4	Geldenhuys
11	McLean	5	van Zyl
10	Burton	6	Zanni
9	Semenzato	7	Favaro
		8	**Parisse**

GRAHAM TIMING

Wales

Try	2	PenTry	0
Conversions		1 / 2	
Penalty Goals		4 / 4	
Drop Goals		0 / 0	

Phases of Play

Scrums Won	4
Lost	0
Lineouts Won	13
Lost	1
Pens Conceded	13
Freekick Conceded	2
Mauls Won	3
Ruck and Drive	22
Ruck and Pass	71

Ball Won

In Open Play	96
In Opponent's 22	38
At Set Pieces	29
Turnovers Won	3

Team Statistics

Passes Completed	210
Line Breaks	4
Possession Kicked	22
Errors from Kicks	1
Kicks to Touch	1
Percentage Kicks	28%
Tackles Made	62
Missed	1
Tackle Completion	98%
Offloads in Tackle	9
Offloads / Tackled	7%
Total Errors Made	12
Errors / Possession	15%

Minutes in Possession

1	13:39	2	16:32

Mins in Opponent's Half

1	28:02	2	26:41

Timeline

Event	Time	Event
HALFPENNY - Penalty	09:26	
	12:08	MI BERGAMASCO - Penalty
HALFPENNY - Penalty	19:43	
HALFPENNY - Penalty	36:56	
	HT	
	48:18	Staibano on for Cittadini
ROBERTS - Try	49:34	
HALFPENNY - Conversion	50:39	
	51:03	Bortolami on for Van Zyl
	52:46	D'Apice on for Ghiraldini
HALFPENNY - Sin Bin	61:37	
Owens on for Rees	62:16	
Charteris on for A W Jones	62:16	
	62:16	Barbieri on for Favaro
R P Jones on for Faletau	62:42	
	65:46	Botes on for Semenzato
	65:46	Benvenuti on for Canale
M S Williams on for J J V Davies	68:14	
PRIESTLAND - Penalty	69:58	
James on for A R Jones	70:12	
	70:40	Toniolatti on for Masi
Webb on for Phillips	70:43	
	71:29	Cittadini on for Lo Cicero
Hook on for Halfpenny	75:10	
CUTHBERT - Try	77:08	
PRIESTLAND - ConMiss	78:29	

Italy

Try	0	PenTry	0
Conversions		0 / 0	
Penalty Goals		1 / 1	
Drop Goals		0 / 0	

Phases of Play

Scrums Won	3
Lost	0
Lineouts Won	13
Lost	3
Pens Conceded	12
Freekick Conceded	1
Mauls Won	3
Ruck and Drive	15
Ruck and Pass	33

Ball Won

In Open Play	51
In Opponent's 22	10
At Set Pieces	29
Turnovers Won	3

Team Statistics

Passes Completed	104
Line Breaks	1
Possession Kicked	25
Errors from Kicks	1
Kicks to Touch	4
Percentage Kicks	30%
Tackles Made	121
Missed	15
Tackle Completion	88%
Offloads in Tackle	4
Offloads / Tackled	6%
Total Errors Made	11
Errors / Possession	13%

Minutes in Possession

1	08:26	2	12:35

Mins in Opponent's Half

1	11:35	2	12:53

Match Facts are recorded under the guidance and direction of STEPHEN P SMITH (WRU REFEREE)

10.03.12 | 16:36

MILLENNIUM STADIUM - 17.03.12

15	Halfpenny	1	Jenkins
14	Cuthbert	2	Rees
13	JJV Davies	3	A R Jones
12	Roberts	4	A W Jones
11	North	5	Evans
10	Priestland	6	Lydiate
9	Phillips	7	**Warburton**
		8	Faletau

WALES 16 — FRANCE 9

	15	Poitrenaud	1	Poux
	14	Fofana	2	Servat
	13	Rougerie	3	Attoub
	12	Fritz	4	Pape
	11	Palisson	5	Maestri
	10	Beauxis	6	**Dusautoir**
	9	Yachvili	7	Bonnaire
			8	Harinordoquy

10	HT	3

GRAHAM TIMING

Try	1	PenTry	0
Conversions		1 / 1	
Penalty Goals		3 / 5	
Drop Goals		0 / 2	

Try	0	PenTry	0
Conversions		0 / 0	
Penalty Goals		3 / 3	
Drop Goals		0 / 2	

Time	Wales	France
0:41		BEAUXIS - DropMiss
11:09		YACHVILI - Penalty
15:37	PRIESTLAND - PenMiss	
21:00	CUTHBERT - Try	
21:59	HALFPENNY - Conversion	
32:15	HALFPENNY - Penalty	
35:39		Buttin on for Poitrenaud
40:52	HALFPENNY - PenMiss	
HT		
40:03	R P Jones on for Warburton	
42:12	PRIESTLAND - DropMiss	
44:04		Debaty on for Poux
44:07		Szarzewski on for Servat
44:26		BEAUXIS - Penalty
47:32		BEAUXIS - DropMiss
52:40	HALFPENNY - Penalty	
53:31		Trinh-Duc on for Palisson
53:37	M S Williams on for JJV Davies	
59:08		Picamoles on for Bonnaire
59:54	JJV Davies on for M S Williams	
63:14	Charteris on for A W Jones	
63:14	Owens on for Rees	
63:14	L D Williams on for Phillips	
67:32		Pierre on for Pape
71:56		Parra on for Beauxis
73:02		YACHVILI - Penalty
75:37	HALFPENNY - Penalty	
78:12	PRIESTLAND - DropMiss	

Phases of Play

	Wales		France
Scrums Won	2		1
Lost	0		0
Lineouts Won	14		9
Lost	3		1
Pens Conceded	10		13
Freekick Conceded	2		4
Mauls Won	1		2
Ruck and Drive	54		25
Ruck and Pass	51		26

Ball Won

	Wales		France
In Open Play	106		53
In Opponent's 22	15		15
At Set Pieces	29		20
Turnovers Won	3		3

Team Statistics

	Wales		France
Passes Completed	164		99
Line Breaks	1		0
Possession Kicked	35		32
Errors from Kicks	1		3
Kicks to Touch	1		10
Percentage Kicks	42%		38%
Tackles Made	69		113
Missed	7		9
Tackle Completion	90%		92%
Offloads in Tackle	3		6
Offloads / Tackled	2%		8%
Total Errors Made	9		16
Errors / Possession	10%		19%

Minutes in Possession

1	19:35	2	17:47

1	13:52	2	13:51

Mins in Opponent's Half

1	26:49	2	23:09

1	14:51	2	21:03

Match Facts are recorded under the guidance and direction of STEPHEN P SMITH (WRU REFEREE)

TEAM PERFORMANCES

TACKLES MADE
ENGLAND	504
WALES	502
FRANCE	493
IRELAND	473
ITALY	448
SCOTLAND	445

MISSED TACKLES
ENGLAND	45
WALES	42
ITALY	40
SCOTLAND	40
IRELAND	38
FRANCE	35

TACKLE COMPLETION
FRANCE	93%
IRELAND	93%
WALES	92%
ENGLAND	92%
ITALY	92%
SCOTLAND	92%

OFF-LOADS IN THE TACKLE
SCOTLAND	51
FRANCE	37
ITALY	34
WALES	32
IRELAND	26
ENGLAND	20

PASSES COMPLETED
SCOTLAND	939
WALES	863
FRANCE	686
ITALY	671
IRELAND	647
ENGLAND	581

POSSESSION KICKED
ENGLAND	136
WALES	127
IRELAND	112
ITALY	112
FRANCE	109
SCOTLAND	92

KICKS / POSSESSION WON
IRELAND	42%
ENGLAND	40%
WALES	39%
ITALY	36%
FRANCE	35%
SCOTLAND	30%

BALL WON IN OPP 22
SCOTLAND	120
IRELAND	117
WALES	110
ITALY	72
FRANCE	62
ENGLAND	40

LINE BREAKS
IRELAND	20
WALES	17
SCOTLAND	15
FRANCE	15
ENGLAND	10
ITALY	10

ERRORS MADE
ENGLAND	59
ITALY	59
FRANCE	57
SCOTLAND	54
IRELAND	50
WALES	44

TURNOVERS WON
ITALY	23
IRELAND	22
ENGLAND	21
FRANCE	21
SCOTLAND	17
WALES	16

RUCK CLEARANCES
ENGLAND	82%
SCOTLAND	82%
ITALY	74%
IRELAND	70%
WALES	67%
FRANCE	66%

SCRUMS WON : LOST
FRANCE	30 : 0
SCOTLAND	24 : 1
ENGLAND	24 : 3
IRELAND	18 : 3
ITALY	18 : 1
WALES	14 : 0

LINEOUTS WON : LOST
WALES	56 : 12
ENGLAND	51 : 7
ITALY	50 : 9
SCOTLAND	50 : 8
FRANCE	46 : 7
IRELAND	33 : 7

PENS CONCEDED : AWARDED
WALES	55 : 53
IRELAND	54 : 40
SCOTLAND	52 : 50
ITALY	49 : 53
ENGLAND	48 : 47
FRANCE	33 : 48

MAULS WON
ENGLAND	22
FRANCE	21
ITALY	20
IRELAND	17
SCOTLAND	14
WALES	8

POINTS SCORED
IRELAND	121
WALES	109
FRANCE	101
ENGLAND	98
SCOTLAND	56
ITALY	53

TRIES FOR : AGAINST
IRELAND	13 : 8
WALES	10 : 3
FRANCE	8 : 8
ENGLAND	7 : 4
SCOTLAND	4 : 11
ITALY	4 : 12

CONVERSIONS
IRELAND	10
WALES	7
ENGLAND	6
FRANCE	5
ITALY	3
SCOTLAND	3

STRIKE RATE
ENGLAND	82%
IRELAND	78%
SCOTLAND	76%
WALES	70%
FRANCE	70%
ITALY	52%

17.03.12

19:10

LEADING SCORERS

POINTS SCORERS	
Leigh Halfpenny (Wal)	66
Owen Farrell (Eng)	63
Jonathan Sexton (Ire)	56
Greig Laidlaw (Sco)	33
Morgan Parra (Fra)	27
Tommy Bowe (Ire)	25
Wesley Fofana (Fra)	20
Kristopher Burton (Ita)	19
Dimitri Yachvili (Fra)	16
Lionel Beauxis (Fra)	15
Alex Cuthbert (Wal)	15
Rory Best (Ire)	10
Jonathan Davies (Wal)	10
Charlie Hodgson (Eng)	10
Andrew Trimble (Ire)	10
Giovanbattista Venditti (Ita)	10
Tobias Botes (Ita)	8
Mirco Bergamasco (Ita)	6
Dan Parks (Sco)	6
Tommaso Benvenuti (Ita)	5
Vincent Clerc (Fra)	5
Tom Court (Ire)	5
Tom Croft (Eng)	5
Keith Earls (Ire)	5
Ben Foden (Eng)	5
Richie Gray (Sco)	5
Stuart Hogg (Sco)	5
Lee Jones (Sco)	5
Julien Malzieu (Fra)	5
Fergus McFadden (Ire)	5
Maxime Medard (Fra)	5
George North (Wal)	5
Sergio Parisse (Ita)	5
Eoin Reddan (Ire)	5
Jamie Roberts (Wal)	5

TRY SCORERS	
Tommy Bowe (Ire)	5
Wesley Fofana (Fra)	4
Alex Cuthbert (Wal)	3
Rory Best (Ire)	2
Jonathan Davies (Wal)	2
Leigh Halfpenny (Wal)	2
Charlie Hodgson (Eng)	2
Andrew Trimble (Ire)	2
Giovanbattista Venditti (Ita)	2
Tommaso Benvenuti (Ita)	2
Vincent Clerc (Fra)	1
Tom Court (Ire)	1
Tom Croft (Eng)	1
Keith Earls (Ire)	1
Ben Foden (Eng)	1
Richie Gray (Sco)	1
Stuart Hogg (Sco)	1
Lee Jones (Sco)	1
Greig Laidlaw (Sco)	1
Julien Malzieu (Fra)	1
Fergus McFadden (Ire)	1
Maxime Medard (Fra)	1
George North (Wal)	1
Sergio Parisse (Ita)	1
Eoin Reddan (Ire)	1
Jamie Roberts (Wal)	1
Aurelien Rougerie (Fra)	1
Manu Tuilagi (Eng)	1
Scott Williams (Wal)	1
Ben Youngs (Eng)	1

GOAL SCORERS	
Owen Farrell (Eng)	23
Jonathan Sexton (Ire)	22
Leigh Halfpenny (Wal)	21
Greig Laidlaw (Sco)	10
Morgan Parra (Fra)	10
Dimitri Yachvili (Fra)	6
Kristopher Burton (Ita)	5
Lionel Beauxis (Fra)	4
Tobias Botes (Ita)	3
Mirco Bergamasco (Ita)	2
Dan Parks (Sco)	2
Julien Dupuy (Fra)	1
Rhys Priestland (Wal)	1
Duncan Weir (Sco)	1

TEAMS	Try	Pts
IRELAND	13	121
WALES	10	109
FRANCE	8	101
ENGLAND	7	98
SCOTLAND	4	56
ITALY	4	53

TOP STRIKE RATE			
Dan Parks (Sco)	2	2	100
Duncan Weir (Sco)	1	1	100
Leigh Halfpenny (Wal)	21	25	84
Owen Farrell (Eng)	23	28	82
Jonathan Sexton (Ire)	22	28	78
Dimitri Yachvili (Fra)	6	8	75
Morgan Parra (Fra)	10	14	71
Kristopher Burton (Ita)	5	7	71
Greig Laidlaw (Sco)	10	14	71
Lionel Beauxis (Fra)	4	6	66
Julien Dupuy (Fra)	1	2	50
Mirco Bergamasco (Ita)	2	4	50
Tobias Botes (Ita)	3	8	37